Praise for THE PLAYBOOK

I'm truly impressed with Christopher Bass's *The Playbook on Fixing Anemic Sales Pipelines, Volume 1: Prospecting*. This book is a very easy read, filled with vital information that inspired me to not only keeping reading, but to implement Christopher's methods IMMEDIATELY.

I would definitely include *The Playbook on Fixing Anemic Sales Pipelines, Volume 1: Prospecting* as one of my top ten favorite books. I will refer this book to my business associates as a MUST read!

Rhonda Gregory Brent – Business Owner

Although I am new to sales, I think *The Playbook on Fixing Anemic Sales Pipelines, Volume 1: Prospecting* gives very practical instruction. It is easy to understand, but at the same time supplies readers with insight into other advice from experts in this field.

Betty Romero – NBC Universal

What I like most about *The Playbook on Fixing Anemic Sales Pipelines, Volume 1: Prospecting* is Christopher Bass's simple-to-understand approach that anyone can apply. This is valuable information.

Saffouh Dabboussi – Dabboussi Insurance Services, Inc.

Wow! I want more! Christopher Bass's *The Playbook on Fixing Anemic Sales Pipelines, Volume 1: Prospecting* is very interesting and thought provoking, invigorating the reader (sales person) to be better. I have attended Christopher's valuable workshops and from those I could not have expected anything less in his book. *The Playbook on Fixing Anemic Sales Pipelines, Volume 1: Prospecting* will definitely enhance your career as salesperson.

Aurora Ramirez– Pre-Need Counselor, Dignity Memorial

Absolutely spot on! I have read a number of books on sales over my fifteen-year career, and I can say Christopher Bass's *The Playbook on Fixing Anemic Sales Pipelines, Volume 1: Prospecting* hits home on many points. No matter if you are new to sales or have been in sales for a while, this is a must read for anyone looking to substantially drive more top line revenue.

Clay Warren – VP Sales, Data Pipeline, Inc.

In an industry that is considered one of the toughest and has a high early burn-out rate, there is a reason Christopher Bass has over twenty years of experience in sales, and has become anexpert andhighly sought-after sales trainer. Get ready to do some highlighting and underlining as Christopher Bass walks you through his tested and proven steps that take anyone from nurturing prospects to closing a deal. Whether you are new to sales and need to absorb all you can, or you are a seasoned professional reading this material for a brush-up, there is something here for everyone. You will learn how to define your target (what works, and what doesn't), how to open doors and move through the process, timing, words to use, who to talk to, and how to navigate your own and your prospects' pain points. But most importantly, if you replicate the guidance in Christopher's book, you WILL close more sales.

Gabriella Sande Waterman – Owner, GSW Financial Partners

In *The Playbook on Fixing Anemic Sales Pipelines, Volume 1: Prospecting* I really like how Christopher Bass deconstructsthe sales process and focuses on lead generation and prospecting. Coming from a professional sales background myself, I appreciate how Christopher breaks lead generation and sales down into parts and then speaks to each part, making his process a great tool for sales teams, as well as entrepreneurs. Christopher's book is to sales what a blueprint is for an architect.

Patti Smith – Innovative Coaching, LLC

When Christopher Bass teaches, you want more. His direct, no-nonsense style engages my thinking in a way I rarely encounter. You will absorb the plethora of insights *The Playbook on Fixing Anemic Sales Pipelines, Volume 1: Prospecting* has to offer, from start to finish. Definitely a must read for anyone in lead generation and sales!

Adrian Harper – CEO, Cloud 77

THE PLAYBOOK

on Fixing Anemic Sales Pipelines

Volume I: Prospecting

THE PLAYBOOK

on Fixing Anemic Sales Pipelines

Volume I: Prospecting

By Christopher Bass MBA

Surrogate Press®

Published in the United States by
Surrogate Press®
an imprint of Faceted Press®
Surrogate Press, LLC
SurrogatePress.com

ISBN: 978-1-947459-14-4

Library of Congress Control Number: 2018938742

Cover design by: Shawn Kelly, *kellygraphicdesign.com*

Interior design by: Katie Mullaly, Surrogate Press®

Table of Contents

Acknowledgments

Writing a book is never a solo endeavor. It is more like a team sport. At least that is what I learned in writing this book, which would not have been possible without the help, advice, and expertise of some very special people.

First let me thank Stacy Dymalski, my editor and one of the main reasons I decide to write this book as opposed to the many others books I had in mind. Stacy attended one of my sales seminars in 2017. Post event, Stacy informed me that she received so much value from the event, that if I had a book for sale she would have purchased it. This sentiment was echoed by many other participants. From that point on, I participated in two of her writing workshops and used her great editing skills to produce this book you have in your hands today.

Next let me give a very special thanks to Katie Mullaly, my publisher at Surrogate Press. Katie provided me with a level of value that will forever serve as the standard in what I expect in working with any publisher. Whether it was all the practical advice she gave me, the responsiveness to my millions of questions, or access to additional resources to help me achieve success with my first book, I thank you, Katie, for all this and much more.

Of course, let me thank Shawn Kelly for a fantastic book cover. I am sure that during the process I was a real pain in the butt.

I want to thank John Harvey for indulging me countless times by letting me bounce ideas and concepts off him to see if they made sense to someone other than myself. I also want to thank my twelve-year-old son, Christopher Santiago Bass, for always asking me how my book was going, debating me on how I should reword certain parts, yet always telling me that he thought my writing was great.

I also want to thank a very special person, Lumi Mesesan. She is a one-of-a-kind person who has constantly given me the most support and encouragement in so many ways. And who also spent countless hours listening to me, re-reading these pages, and making great suggestions on how I could make this book fundamentally better. Thank you!

Finally, to all my past employers, past and current clients, and friends whom I have helped achieve better sales results; I thank you. Had it not been for you and the thousands of real-life situations and challenges I experienced with you, I would not have learned as much as I have, and therefore, would not have developed the expertise which serves as the foundation of this book.

Introduction

To find or to be found, that is the question. Or at least that sounded great when I thought about it. In all seriousness, this does seem to be the great debate of our time when it comes to how to build a pipeline of qualified prospects. You might be more familiar with the framing of this debate with such terms as inbound marketing vs. outbound prospecting. While I understand the premises of each side of the debate, my practical question, "does it matter"?

Consider this situation. If you are hunting for food to feed your family, wouldn't you capture your target more efficiently and effectively if you use bait? Of course! But what if you had no effective bait, or what if the target does not take the bait, what would you do? Would you sit there all day waiting? Or would you go out looking for that target?

Let's consider fishing. My grandfather is an avid fisherman. While I have never gone on a fishing trip with him, I have often heard him speak about the importance of using the right bait. What would happen if you had the wrong bait or if you were unsuccessful in your quest to catch any fish for your family to eat?

The answers to any of the above questions depend on how much your family needed food, or how much help you had in capturing this food, or even what your resources or tools you possessed. Now, I don't hunt nor fish for my food. I simply go to the local grocery store and purchase my food. Be that as it may, my point here should be obvious. I don't see the pragmatism in this debate, because from my experience it is not a question of either or, but rather one of both. Because depending upon your unique set of circumstances, and unless you are going to go out and buy "qualified prospects" for your pipeline, (which is a viable option for many companies both small and large) one way of getting qualified prospects may in fact be better than the other. However, in most situations, a combination approach of inbound and outbound is the best "broad strategy" for efficaciously generating qualified prospects for your empty pipeline.

Granted, I know that my fundamentally sound points above will not cease this debate. One can only try! While I understand that this book is more about finding qualified prospects rather than having them find you, my aim is to help you, the reader, open your mind and expand your options to include strategies from both inbound marketing and outbound prospecting in your quest to generate more qualified opportunities. This is extremely more important in that it has become progressively difficult to do so for many businesses.

Laying the Foundation

PART I

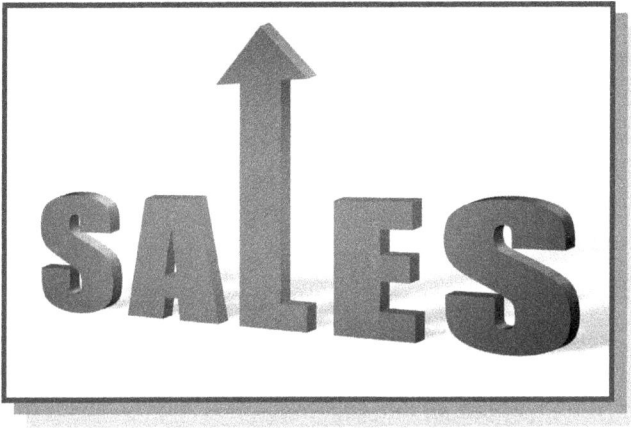

1: Sales

I am not judged by the number of times I fail, but by the number of times I succeed; and the number of times I succeed is in direct proportion to the number of times I can fail and keep on trying.

– TOM HOPKINS –

When I first started my selling career nearly twenty years ago, I learned that sales was nothing more than a transaction between the seller and the prospective buyer where money (or something with a monetary value) is exchanged for goods or services. Great definition, right? But is there more? Depending on the source, the answer to that question varies. Sales may be defined simply as the activity or business of selling products or services.[1] Mike Kaplan in his book *Secrets of a Master Closer* defines sales as the act of "persuading or convincing" someone to buy your product, your service or idea.[2] At the writing of this book, I reached out to the National Association of Sales Professional (NASP) and the National Sales Network (NSN) to determine if any of the two organizations had developed a formal definition of sales. On its website, the NASP states that it is the number one resource for sales professionals.[3] Similarly, the NSN is a 501(c)(3) not-for-profit membership organization whose objective is to meet the professional and development needs of sales and sales management professionals and individuals who want to improve their professional sales skills.[4] The NASP is also an association for career salespeople. It offers a certification program called the CPSP, Certified Professional Salesperson. I rightly assumed that if anyone had a formal definition of sales, it would be these two organizations. At the time this book was published, however, I have not received a response from either. In his book *Be Obsessed or Be Average*, Grant Cardone states that sales is more than a department and more than someone's job. Sales is the god of any business.[5] Bold Statement? Yes! Regardless of any formal definition, one thing is very clear. Sales is highly important, critically important, in many ways.

The Importance of Sales

You might ask how important? Well consider these statistics. Eighty percent of new startups fail within the first year. Of the remaining 20%, half fail before the fifth year. Wow! Yes, let me repeat. Of the remaining 20% of new startups that survive the first year of being in business, half fail before the fifth-year mark. You think this is alarming, consider this number. Only 6% of the businesses that started out ten years ago, are still operational. The other 94% have closed their doors long before the tenth year.

Of course, there have been many studies conducted articulating the *Whys*. Essentially, it is my conclusion that all reasons boil down to two major factors. The first is lack of access to capital. Sadly, most small businesses do not have the connections, the credit history, or the collateral necessary to get the capital to start and sustain the working cash flow requirements of their businesses. But even if they could, such a move would be a mistake according to Mark Cuban. In 2013, in an interview with a reporter from *Bloomberg*, Mark is quoted saying, "Only morons start a small business on a loan."[6] Is he right? Regardless of whether you agree or disagree with Cuban's statement, there is a second reason more impactful at play.

Let's say the business owner gets the loan. How will the loan be repaid? The answer is simple. The business owner repays the loan and covers all the other immediate cash flows needs by generating sales. Yes, that is right. It is the failure to generate enough sales that causes the majority of businesses to fail. Stated another way. Far too many businesses fail because not enough customers buy products in large enough quantities and at margins high enough to ensure survivability. Guess what? If a company does not continue to grow new revenue, then it shrinks. No sales; no profits; no business; period!

As a Sales Profession

Businesses need salespeople to bring in the revenue it needs to start up, operate, normalize and grow. It does not matter if the business has one salesperson or hundreds. It does not matter if that one person is the owner or any number of people. It does not matter if that person has an official title of salesperson. None of these things matter. What does matter is the simple fact that a business needs someone who is primarily responsible for generating sales. Thus, if sales is the foundation for business success, and if the sales professional is the one primarily tasked with generating sales, is there any doubt of just how important this sales role is? After all, learning how to generate sales at a high level is what most sales professionals are charged to execute everyday.

In Life and Business

As vitally important as the sales role is to a business, the ability to sell is equally important in other roles in an organization and to other aspects of our lives. This is especially true whenever we are seeking to get "what we want" and where the attainment of "what we want" involves another person's willing participation. Learning how to sell is, therefore, equally important in non-sales roles such as selling people that your ideas and concepts make sense and they should adopt them, or to move them to take a course of action. Yeah, I know what you are probably thinking right now. You have heard this statement many times before, and frankly you don't buy it. Before you write me off forever, I ask you to consider the following situations as proof.

Maybe you are trying to negotiate better lease terms on a car or apartment. Maybe you are a parent attempting to "sell" your kids on the idea of doing homework or taking a bath. Maybe you are a teacher striving to persuade your students on the value of an education. Maybe you are a lawyer selling the jury on the innocence of your client. Maybe you are a politician tasked with convincing her constituents on the value of a piece of legislation. Maybe you are an entrepreneur needing to raise venture capital and need to "sell" the potential investor on not just investing, but accepting your terms, as well. Maybe you need to convince your supplier to deliver a much-needed shipment of supplies. Whatever the situation, failure to master selling skills means you lose. You lose in getting your way in life. You lose in failing to influence the outcome of others' decisions. You lose in convincing people to willingly do what you desire.

Success in generating sales, be it new business or existing business, boils down to being successful at two things.

1. A sales professional must be successful at generating enough qualified leads, or qualified opportunities (i.e. prospects, sales ready opportunities).

2. The salesperson must be successful in converting a large percentage of those prospects into paying customers.

Eventually, for the business to be sustainable, there is also the post-sales or delivery and service component to this conversation. Such a discussion, unfortunately, is outside the primary scope of this book. Be ever mindful, that failure in any of the first two ultimately results in failure of the business.

There have been many books written over the years about sales, lead generation, prospecting, closing, etc. My aim in writing this book is not to replace any of these great works. Instead, I aspire to take the lessons I have learned from those books, plus the twenty-plus years of selling as a professional and the thirteen-plus years of managing, coaching, and training other sales professionals and synthesize it all into a practical, easy to understand, simple to execute framework so you can become not just great at prospecting, but ultimately become a prospecting machine!

What is Social Selling?

In the age of the Internet, the term Social Selling has emerged. While I generally don't use this term very often when I speak or train, I do use many aspects of Social Selling, especially when it comes to prospecting. With this disclosure, permit me to do a little defining of this term. Social Selling is often defined as using the various social networks to find, connect with and nurture prospects so that when it comes time to buy, these prospects are already familiar with your brand. Thus, making the buying decision easier and faster. Similarly, LinkedIn defines Social Selling as "leveraging your social network to find the right prospects, build trusted relationships, and ultimately, achieve your sales goals."[7]

You may be asking why did I include a brief discussion of Social Selling in the first few pages of this book? Am I one of those "enlightened ones" who believe in the hype, the buzz, regarding how Social Selling is taking over, making traditional aspects of selling increasingly obsolete?

The obvious answer is no, I don't believe in the hype. However, I know from personal experience that Social Selling has become a vital tool for helping us gain insights, making connections and building relationships with prospects faster than it had been previously possible. Because of this understanding, I have decided to dedicate a significant amount of time on this subject later in this book. For now, let's jump right into getting an understanding of the broader topic of lead generation.

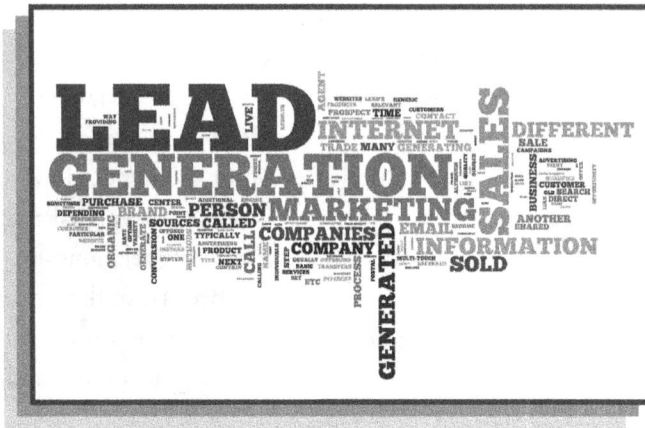

2: Lead Generation

By far the most efficient approach to deal with your leads is always to use a process that automatically brands you, supplies worth to your prospects, follows up with them, and sorts out the uninterested people.

– CALLBOX INC –

Jeffrey Gitomer is famous for saying, nothing happens until a sale is made. While this is absolutely true, without a lead, no sale can take place, however. This meaning is simple. If sales is the driver of economic movement, then leads are its fuel. If sales is the grand building towering over the city, then leads are its foundation. If sales is the head on the body, then leads is its neck. Thus, lead generation is the single most important element in generating sales and ensuring business survivability.

According to Marketo, a leading marketing automation platform, lead generation "describes the marketing process of stimulating and capturing interest in a product or service for developing sales pipeline. As the buying process has changed, marketers need to find new ways to reach buyers and get heard through the noise. Instead of finding customers with mass advertising and email blasts, marketers must now focus on being found and learn to build continuous relationships with buyers."[1] I assert that Lead Generation is much more than that. Lead generation include both the inbound marketing process described by Marketo, but it also includes that universe of goals, strategies, tactics and processes for piquing prospect interest and converting that interest into qualified opportunities for the funnel. These sales opportunities must ultimately result in new customers. Regardless of whether you accept my definition or Marketo's definition, lead generation is clearly a process that requires preparation, precision and persistence.

Two Broad Approaches to Lead Generation

Over the years, I have come to conclude and accept that there are generally only two major ways of generating leads.

1. Promotion
2. Prospecting

Because of this distinction, I have often been tasked with clearly defining promotion relative to or versus prospecting. When you think about it, promoting and prospecting are both outbound efforts that a company or sales professional pursue. There are, nevertheless, some subtle differences. For instance, promotion is tasked with generating enough awareness, enough interest, enough demand that the buyer initiates the all-important sales conversation. In other words, promotion is used to attract prospects. While prospecting seeks to achieve the same goals, it does so with the intention of the sales professional initiating this same all-important sales conversation. This means that prospecting is about finding and discovering prospects. To reiterate, promotion results in the buyer initiating the sales conversation while prospecting results in the sales professional initiating this conversation. Promotion is about attracting while prospecting is about finding. Is one better than the other? Is one a better fit for a particular company? A particular type of product? A particular type of salesperson? Depends, depends and depends again.

Many inside sales organizations in the SaaS (software-as-a-service) space, plus other companies from a host of different industries, increasingly rely more on the promotion approach to lead generation and are moving away from prospecting. This is due in part to the evolution of the seller-buyer relationship and the challenges associated with perfecting an effective outbound prospecting strategy. While I do understand the environmental factors that have caused this shift, I do believe that such a move is short-sighted. I don't believe that this conversation is one of either or, but instead one of both. Hence, part of my mission is to explain why prospecting is still a viable option especially for those companies suffering from anemic prospect pipelines.

Promotion

If you were to look up the meaning of promotion in the American Marketing Association Online Dictionary, you would find the term being defined as "coordinated promotional messages and related media used to communicate with a market."[2] Whenever you promote your business, you answer a few key questions.

1. How do I get known by my target market?
2. Where do I need to be (location, presence and exposure wise) so that my target market can find me and find my message?
3. Once found, what is the message that will resonate with the buyer so that he will "want" to do business with me?

At the end of the day, you want to effectively communicate your values to your potential buyers, because remember, if potential customers don't have a compelling reason for selecting you over another vendor of equal quality and comparable pricing, then they won't. You also need to ensure you are clear on the goal(s) of your promotional effort and whether or not you should promote. And finally, you must make informed decisions about the various communicational or promotional channels you will use in order to motivate buyers to initiate these all-important sales conversations. Such a deep dive on the topic of promotion is beyond the scope of this book. I know. I know. I know. I am sorry to have to disappoint. However, what is within the scope of this book is a detail discussion on prospecting, the second major way of generating leads.

3: Prospecting

Prospecting in not the mystery many people make it out to be!

– MARK HUNTER –

Prospecting (often identified as the first step in the "direct" sales process) consists of identifying potential customers (prospects) and contacting and engaging with these prospects in the hopes that they are qualified enough to do business with you. A colleague of mine, often stresses how prospecting is the art and science of developing new relationships and creating new opportunities that later turn into sales. Many in the formal school of marketing might refer to prospecting as being a subset of direct marketing or to it being nothing more than a direct promotion channel of marketing. While the later makes sense academically, I don't think it makes sense practically to view prospecting as just an extension of promotion.

Prospecting is different from promotion in the sense that with promoting we look to generate buyer-initiated sales conversations, whereas with prospecting we look to have sales professionals initiate these sales conversations. In promoting we wait for the buyer to come to us; in prospecting, we don't wait for them to come to use. We go to them. These points might seem to be common and obvious. However, this is not always the case. Recently I read an article by Richard Stephens a contributor on Hubspot.com who attempted to define "inbound prospecting."[1] That is correct, inbound prospecting. Let me be clear. My position is that if a lead or potential customer initiates contact with a salesperson, this is not prospecting. The buyer-initiated outreach came as a result of some type of promotion done by the company or the sales professional. True, the goal is to qualify the opportunity and move the lead through the same sales process as a prospecting opportunity. However, this so-called "inbound prospecting" process might better be referred to as "inbound lead qualification."

The Goal of Prospecting

With prospecting, the ultimate goal is to find or discover a potential buyer, a qualified lead, or a sales opportunity that you can work and win. You are looking for prospects that have unfulfilled goals you can help them attain; desires you can help them fulfill; pain you can help them ease; challenges you can help them address; needs you can help them satisfy; or problems you can help them solve. This is a critical point to understand. If a suspect, (a contact who you believe may fit all your ideal client factors) with whom you have engaged in a qualifying conversation has no pain, has no need, has no problem, then this suspect will never be a qualified lead until such a challenge arise. By the same token, if the lead does have a need or pain that you normally help address, but for which you have no solution, then this lead also would not be a prospect and should be excluded from any further prospecting efforts. Granted, you may elect to develop referral relationships with other providers who might be able to help. Nonetheless, for your own sales funnel, this type of lead is not a prospect for you. Interestingly though, a fair number of contacts you engage with during your prospecting activities will not be a prospect for you no matter how hard you try.

Suspect versus Prospect

Pick up any book on sales and invariably there will be a discussion regarding suspects versus prospects. That is, what is a suspect, and what is a prospect? David Mattson, in his book entitled *The Sandler Rules* defines suspect as a contact with whom you might be able to sell to, but with whom you have not connected with in any way.[2] If you read any of Stephen Schiffman's books, he defines prospects as people who progress with you through the steps of the sales process and who are going to "play ball with you."[3] While both of these statements are good, I don't believe they are good enough.

Essentially, the key difference in determining who is a prospect or suspect, boils down to whether or not you have had a qualify conversation. That is to say, all contacts, all leads, are suspects until you have had that all-important qualification conversation. For the record, a "contact or lead" is a name with details like: full name, address, phone number, email address, etc. It can be a standalone contact, or it can be a contact within a targeted company, which at the surface fits some demographic profile. Because of this profile match, you suspect this contact might be a prospect, but you don't know for sure and won't know until you can get into a qualifying conversation to make this determination. I often hear sales professionals debate qualified leads versus qualified prospects, or sales-ready opportunities versus qualified potential, or potential customer versus prospective buyer. Let me do my best to clear up this confusion. Definitively, the goal of prospecting is to generate prospects. Stated another way, the goal of prospecting is to generate qualified leads or sales-ready opportunities. These sales opportunities are only opportunities because the potential buyer fits all factors for your ideal target. This is true regardless of what you call the targets.

Four Major Steps to Prospecting

By now it should be clear that prospecting is tasked with proactively generating qualified leads. In order to be successful in attaining this goal, there are four major steps that a salesperson must execute; **Find; Contact; Engage; and Qualify.** I will cover these steps later in the book. For now, however, be mindful that each step is what we must do to generate prospects. Consequently, each major step has its own set of objectives and necessary sub-steps, which must be executed timely in order to achieve total success.

Two Styles of Prospecting

Continuing this flow of thinking, I now want to discuss what I consider to be the two major styles or methods of prospecting. The first style is *hunting*. Just as the term suggests, a hunting style of prospecting is when you look for qualified opportunities that you can close today or within a relatively short time frame. Think about a door-to-door solar salesperson for a moment; or a telemarketer calling a business to sell SEO services. This style of prospecting is often transactional in nature, with the sales cycle being relatively short; but it could also be complex. A number of hardcore prospectors refer to this style of prospecting as "eating what you kill" that same day.

The second style of prospecting is called *farming*. This is where you find opportunities that while not closable today, can (and hopefully will) close over time with a little nurturing and developing. This style of prospecting has a much longer sales cycle and most often involves the selling of complex solutions. Think of real estate agents, insurance agents, and software sales specialists leveraging this style of prospecting.

Depending on your choice of communication channel, one style of prospecting is better suited than the other. For example, because Social Media Prospecting and Net Prospecting (to be explain in greater details in subsequent chapters) are inherently relationship oriented, a farming style to prospecting works best for these channels. Conversely, if a sales professional is looking to leverage the power of Tele Prospecting and In-Person Prospecting, and if the need for leads and deals is now, then a hunting style of prospecting is more fitting.

The **Whys** for Prospecting

Before getting into a deep discussion on the major prospecting steps, it is important to ask the why question. That is, why do we or should we prospect? I mean, why should we prospect when we have inbound leads, inbound calls, inbound emails, walk in traffic coming straight to us? In this situation, prospecting is not necessary if the company is getting enough buyer-initiated leads. Again, under this circumstance, prospecting is not compulsory. If, however, the inbound lead flow is either not adequate or even non-existent, then prospecting is crucial. Again, prospecting is important and necessary when there is either no inbound leads and/or when the inbound lead flow is not enough. There is a famous saying (so famous that I don't know who originally said it); *If you don't have a stream of potential clients knocking at your door, or if you have some, but not enough (the results of effective promoting), then maybe, just maybe, this is a sign that you need to get out and go prospecting!* To reiterate, prospecting becomes important when there is no leads or not enough inbound leads in the sales pipeline, regardless of the source.

Why Reps Don't Prospect

At this point, it should be safe for me to assume that we are on the same page when it comes to the importance of lead generation and prospecting specifically. By now, it should also be clear how important, *critically important*, prospecting is in closing and winning business. Unfortunately, far too many salespeople either don't prospect or don't prospect enough. This of course leads to the obvious question of "Why?" Is it that the sales professionals do not know how to prospect? Is it that there are no effective systems present to help the salesperson acquire the knowledge, skills or resources necessary to prospect effectively? Is it that prospecting skills are innate, and that if you are not born with this know-how, then you are doomed to failure? While the above reasons might make a great Hollywood movie or a nail biting novel, the two biggest reasons that salespeople fail to prospect boils down to **hate** and **fear**.

Every job that we perform, no matter how important or unimportant, has some parts that we like to do the most and parts we least like to do. Selling is no exception. Most sales professionals, of course, love to qualify, talk features and benefits, demo the product and write the order; but few, and I mean *few*, sales reps like to prospect. I would go as far to say, not only do they not like it, but many sales professionals even *hate* it. Ava Frost[4], a marketer with HubSpot, compiled a report that stated 40% of salespeople, when asked what part of their jobs they found to be the most difficult, pointed to prospecting.

Let's face it. Researching potential targets; making hundreds of calls that go straight to voicemail most of the time; repeatedly hearing "No" and rejections 60%, 70%, or 80% of the time; spending countless hours drafting emails only to have them get blocked by spam filters; being constantly stop by those gatekeepers. I mean this list is endless. Thus, it is no wonder that the average sales professional hates prospecting. It is freaking hard, tedious and seemingly unrewarding.

Additionally, sales professional fear rejection. In their defense, however, it is a commonly known and accepted truism that humans fear rejection. Contrary to what many buyers think, salespeople are humans too. Nonetheless, prospecting and sales are activities in which a high number of rejections are inevitable. Anytime you attempt to influence prospects or buyers to take a particular course of action, or to do something differently, there will be those who reject and push back on your attempts. Some prospects might even push back very forcefully and aggressively. Because of this, many sales professionals refuse to prospect. As profound as hate and fear are in inhibiting a salesperson's ability (and desire) to prospect, there are a few others as well.

In his book *Fanatical Prospecting*, Jeb Blount argues that there are three reasons why salespeople don't prospect; **Procrastination**, **Perfectionism**, and **Paralysis-from-Analysis**.[5] He referred to these as the Three Ps. With Procrastination, the sales professional is always finding reasons to not prospect today; always putting prospecting off, always with the promise of "getting around to it later," but later rarely comes. When the salesperson waits to prospect until the last month, this creates a huge vacuum in his or her pipeline. Consequently, there won't be enough opportunities in the pipeline. As a result, the salesperson does not close enough sales and thus, must prospect more. It's a vicious cycle.

Unlike the Procrastinator who is unwilling to act until the last moment, the Perfectionist acts right now, as long as everything is perfect. If all is not perfect, then he or she suddenly does not have all the answers. It's always something; doesn't have all the right materials, isn't working in the perfect environment, doesn't have all the possible information about the prospect. If all is not perfect, then he or she will not act. Unfortunately, rarely will everything be perfect. Thus, like the Procrastinator, the Perfectionist gets very little prospecting done.

And finally, the Paralysis-by-Analysis salesperson has roots in perfectionism. But here the salesperson fails to prospect because they over analyze every situation and every nuisance of every situation, making sure that all their ducks are perfectly aligned before acting. What they fail to realize is that rarely will all their ducks be perfectly aligned. Again, the net result, no prospecting.

Overcoming the Tendency to Not Prospect

We have established that prospecting is critical to sales success and business survivability. We have also established that far too many salespeople fail to prospect. We have explored at least five reasons why prospecting does not happen as often as it need to. Remember, if the salesperson does not prospect, **AND** if there are no inbound leads, then there are no opportunities in the funnel. Without opportunities in the funnel, there are no sales. No sales for a business means business failure.

Wow, what a doomsday scenario right? Well, not necessarily. This is easily fixable. Sales professionals just need to prospect more often, more efficiently and more effectively. That stated, how can a sales professional overcome the crippling tendency to not prospect?

The answer to this question is eight-fold.

4: Eight Steps to Becoming Great

... be not afraid of greatness. Some are born great, some achieve greatness, and some have greatness thrust upon 'em.

– WILLIAM SHAKESPEARE –

The first thing a salesperson must accept is the reality that unless he gets good, or better yet – great at prospecting, his or her success in sales will be severely limited. Moreover, his sales career lifespan will be short lived. While you don't have to love prospecting, you do have to **accept the fact that you need to do it** in order to reach high levels of income and career success. In his book *Relentless: From Good, to Great to Unstoppable* Tim Grover, a sport performance expert for elite athletes, speaks about how "Unstoppable Athletes" don't like the grinding hours of practice or the long and painful conditioning, or the thousands of repetitions of the same fundamental. However, they know that in order to experience the lights, the flash, the excitement and the love of fans, plus earn the large paychecks and get those mega endorsement deals, these elite athletes have to accept the "unlikeable and undesirable" and often "loathsome" aspect of training. They must do the unlikable and undesirable work nonetheless.[1] In short, you don't have to like prospecting, but you do have to ultimately do it.

Now if you have to prospect, and make no mistake you do have to prospect, why not do it at a high level? Why not **make the commitment to do it to the best of your ability?** Because doing so only increases the likelihood that you achieve your goals faster and with greater ease. Because doing so helps you become great or unstoppable in prospecting. Because doing so increases your earning power in the immediate sense. Because doing so puts you in a rare category of elite sales professionals, increasing your market value exponentially, which allows you to have whatever job, position, perk, and benefits you want. When this happens, you eventually become the "man" or as some would say, *the rainmaker*.

In addition to accepting prospecting as part of your role and making the commitment to get good or great at it, you also need to **follow a proven system** that provides you with a detailed step-by-step process. Because we call sales a science, or better yet – an art, following a proven system that helps you achieve your goals faster is a brilliant move. And for the record, providing you with such a system is one of the principle goals of this book. Such a proven system enables you to build your prospecting muscles. Like any muscle, the more you use it, the stronger it gets, and the more comfortable and effortless your movements become. Consequently, you get better results thereby boosting our confidence,

Fourthly, **you should make it a habit of counting the "No's."** If you recall, prospecting and sales are activities in which a high number of rejections are inevitable. Interestingly enough, if you do something long enough, you will eventually experience results. If you learn from the mistakes and the missteps, you can learn to experience those results faster. Thus, there is value in hearing "No." Hearing "No" helps you develop a "thick-skin." Hearing "No" helps you overcome the fear of rejection. Hearing "No" forces you to learn how to overcome those "No's." In other words, getting and counting "No's" are essential parts of your sales success. The more "No's" you get, the closer you are to getting a "Yes."

For example, if your qualification rate (appointment set rate to prospect rate) is 10%, this means that for every ten contacts (or leads) you speak with, you generate one appointment or one qualified lead. This also means you got nine No's. You get nine No's on your way to get one Yes (appointment set, qualified lead).

This acceptance of No's as part of the process is a core part of understanding your numbers and realizing that while very few sales professionals like to get rejected or be told no, you also realize that getting your nine No's, means you are on your way to one Yes. Thus, if you need five appointments (or five qualified leads) for your funnel, then you should expect and be prepared (all things being equal and ratios staying consistent) to get forty-five No's.

Understanding the Math

Due to the supremely critical role of prospecting, expert after expert, article after article, study after study have all suggested, argued, and admonished the importance of prospecting. You may now be mentally asking yourself, "OK. I get it. I have to prospect. But how often do I need to? Do I work just on it a few days a week? Or do I prospect all day, every day?"

To answer these questions effectively, you need to know three numbers. You need to **do the math**. This math in question is as follows:

1. Your win rate (prospect to close deal rate)

2. Your qualification rate (contact to prospect rate)

3. The number of close deals you need in a defined period of time

Let's discuss your win rate first. Your win rate (aka close rate) is the number of deals you close relative to the number of prospects you have in your funnel. Stated another way, how many prospects do you need to possess to close one deal? Let's say your close rate is 10%, meaning you close one deal for every ten prospects in your pipeline.

The second ratio is your qualification rate. This is the number of contacts you need to have in your database to generate a prospect. Let's say that number is also 10%. So, for every one deal you win you need ten prospects AND one hundred contacts. Do you follow the math? If you don't, please re-read this part. For everyone deal you win, you need ten qualified leads AND one hundred contacts/leads.

The last piece of math you need to know is the number of deals you desire or need to close in your reporting or quota period. That period could be daily, weekly, monthly, quarterly or annually. Continuing with our example above. Let's say, you need to win ten deals this month. This means for ten deals, you need one hundred prospects, yet to generate one hundred prospects you need to work 1,000 contacts. In other words, if you generated one hundred prospects, and you won ten deals from those prospects, then you would need to work 1,000 prospects during this defined period.

Now, you might be saying to yourself that generating 100 prospects from 1,000 contacts monthly sounds like a lot. I agree with you to an extent. These numbers, however, could be made better by improving your conversion rate of contacts to prospects (qualification rate). So instead of your conversion rate being 10%, let's place it at 20%. That means for ten deals you still need one hundred prospects, but now you only need 500 contacts. This prospecting load could also be lightened by optimizing your close or win rate. Let's say instead of it being 10% that your win rate is 20%, so with ten deals you would need fifty prospects and with the same 20% qualification rate, you would need just 250 contacts. Understanding these numbers are the basis for not just knowing when and how often you should prospect, it also helps set the stage for what your daily activities should be.

The Replacement Value

Continuing this discussion above, if you understand what your numbers are, you will have a better understanding of **your replacement value**. While I have had it explained to me and taught to me in a variety of different ways, in his book *Fanatical Prospecting* Jeb Blount explains it perfectly, albeit, he refers to it as the Law of Replacement.[2] Keep in mind that as you work the leads in your pipeline, one of two things happen; you either win it, or you lose it (or it falls out of your funnel for many reasons). Either way, when leads fall outside your funnel you have to replace them. This replacement, however, is not a one-to-one relationship. Just because you won or lost one lead does not mean that you replace it with just one lead. No! Instead you need to replenish based on your closing ratio. Continuing this 10% win rate scenario, for every ten prospects in your funnel, you close one. Therefore, when you win one, you have to replace it with ten more. Why ten more? Why not just one? Well, statistically, there are nine prospects in your pipeline who you will not be able to close; remember your 10% win rate. But because you don't know which nine, you need to replace that one won deal with ten new prospects. Failure to heed this point about replacement is what leads sales reps to alternate between feast and famine.

During the famine, because there is nothing to eat, you spend all your time hunting and gathering all the food you can. Depending upon your skill level and the presence of targets and other foods, this hunting and gathering could take a few days, a few weeks or even a few months. Eventually and historically, when the cupboards are full, you stop hunting and gathering and focus on the feast before you. As you go about your days, eating and rejoicing, you are unaware that the more you eat, the lower your food supplies are getting. So unless you are constantly replacing what you eat, we will find your supplies running out. Eventually, you are back to the famine again and need to hunt.

The Daily Effect

What the replacement value teaches us is that you must constantly prospect regardless of whether you are winning or losing deals. Understanding your math helps you know how many contacts and prospects you need in your pipeline to win the requisite number of sales. Implicit in this discussion is the point of needing to **prospect daily**. Why daily? Well, your sales cycle, the number of deals you win plus the replacement value dictate that you must constantly prospect for new opportunities. Always remember this point. The prospecting you do today, will benefit you within this month, and the prospecting you do this month, will benefit you within the next ninety days. Conversely, failure to prospect today will hurt you this week. Failure to prospect this month will hurt you within the next ninety days.

The aim is to always make the effort to prospect daily. Never put it off for anyone or anything. Because failure to prospect daily will have a negative impact when you least expect it and often when you can't afford it.

Prospecting Effectively and Efficiently

How do you know if you are prospecting effectively? How do you know that you are doing it the right way? The simple answer is when you have qualified leads in your sales funnel. Makes sense, right? Well, this is only part of it. You know you are prospecting effectively when you have the requisite number of prospects or qualified opportunities in your pipeline that are sufficient for you to comfortably hit your sales target. Anything short of that number and you are not prospecting effectively. Unless you replace contacts and prospects that fall outside your funnel, and unless you do this daily, you will eventually find yourself constantly alternating between the feast and famine cycle discussed earlier.

Additionally, you know that you are prospecting effectively when you are both efficient and effective. What does this mean? Prospecting efficiently means you get enough done in the time you have allocated. Prospecting effectiveness is a ratio of activities to outcome. For example, if you made 1,000 calls in a three-hour time block, you would be labeled a highly efficient prospector. Yet, if those 1,000 calls generated zero qualified leads, zero appointments or zero sales, then you would be labeled grossly ineffective. The goal with prospecting is to find the right mix of doing enough activities that get you the desire outcome.

Another way of measuring how great you are at prospecting is to look at your rate of return on qualified leads. In SaaS, there is a term that companies use to determine how effective its prospecting efforts are. This term is known as "Lead Velocity Rate." This simply means a company has a month-over-month increase in the quantity and quality of prospects in its pipeline. If a company is not increasing the quantity, as well as the quality, of prospects it has in pipeline, it will progressively find itself constantly falling short of its sales/revenue quota. It is these factors that a sales professional uses to determine how effective and efficient he or she is in finding, contacting, engaging and qualifying prospects. Before getting into how to execute these four major steps involved in generating qualified leads, I want to first go over the various communication channels that you use to perform these steps.

Selecting the "Best" Communication Channels

PART II

5: Communication Channels

*To effectively communicate we must realize that we are all different
in the way we perceive the world and use this understanding
as a guide to our communication with others.*

– TONY ROBBINS –

N ow you know your mission.

1. Find your targets

2. Contact and engaged your targets

3. Qualify your targets in a way that separates your real prospects
   from mere suspects

Like any profession, there are various tools you have at your disposal. These
are tools will or should aid you in the execution of your mission. One such
major category of tools is the communication channels. These communication
channels are nothing more than the various means of communication available to the organization or the sales professional. I am talking about traditional
channels like: telephone, emailing, direct mail, and in-person visits. This also

includes newer channels like SMS and social media. In order to maximize your efforts, it is advisable to know and understand which communication channels are the most effective for each major step in the prospecting process. What follows is a discussion about each channel. The coverage includes various benefits and disadvantages of each channel, as well as practical steps for effectively leveraging each channel.

6: Tele Prospecting

The telephone, which interrupts the most serious conversations and cuts short the weightiest observation, has a romance of its own.

– VIRGINIA WOOLF –

The telephone, as we know it today, was the creation of Alexander Graham Bell in 1880s. While it was used second only to the telegraph up into the early 1900s, the telephone would eventually become the primary means by which the world communicated over long distances. Even though the shape, size, functions, and usages of the telephone have changed radically over the past twenty years, we still probably take the telephone for granted in our personal lives. This, however, is not the case in the business world. Still to this very day, businesses use the telephone for many reasons, such as prospecting, selling, contract discussion, customer service, collections, medical treatment, conference calls, you name it. The usages and applications for the phone in today's business environments are endless. One use of particular interest is Tele Prospecting.

As complicated as the term may sound, Tele Prospecting is simply the act of prospecting via the phones. It is stated that 80% of salespeople still think the phone is the best communication channel for closing deals. Yet a fair number of those sales professionals are reluctant to use that same phone for prospecting? Why is that? Many sales experts argue that at the root of this reluctance is the phenomenon known as *call reluctance*. In a blog post, Gary Stauble, of The Recruiting Lab, defines call reluctance as "an emotional short circuit that diverts energy from the act of prospecting to the act of procrastinating."[1] What this means is that instead of making calls, call-reluctant salespeople keep themselves busy preparing and avoiding the phone. They allow their fears to stand in the way of their goals and it extracts a high emotional and financial cost.

While the term makes sense for some sales professionals who are hesitant to pick up the phones (or do any outbound prospecting for that matter), some sales reps, however, are simply in the wrong job. Consequently, they should do something other than prospecting, other than cold-calling, other than proactively generating leads.

Benefits of Tele Prospecting

Aside from In-Person Prospecting, there is no faster way of getting into an immediate two-way conversation with the prospect. While many of the other communication channels can be used for finding, contacting, engaging, and nurturing a prospect, there are only two channels where effective qualification of a prospect takes place: In-Person Prospecting and Tele Prospecting. Because you are able to get into a direct conversation with a prospect for qualifying purposes, Tele Prospecting grants one the ability to move leads through the sales funnel faster. This is akin to an assembly line. When you add the unlimited local and long distance calling options included in just about every personal and business phone plan, the cost per call is considerably cheaper than any other prospecting activity. This is especially true when compared to In-Person Prospecting, Direct Mail, and Fax Prospecting.

But all that aside, Tele Prospecting is one of the very best ways of increasing one's visibility and expanding one's reach outside of a local market or territory. Just think about it. If you needed to expand into new markets, and you have a limited amount of time and money to do so, which communication channel would you select? Would you select Direct Mail? Would you select Email Prospecting? Would you select Door-to-Door? No! You would select Tele Prospecting.

Disadvantages of Tele Prospecting

On June 27, 2003, the United States FTC (Federal Trade Commission) set up the National Do- Not-Call Registry. This was done to comply with the Do-Not-Call Implementation Act of 2003 signed into law by President George W. Bush. The intent of the law was to address the mountainous consumer complaints of unwanted solicitation calls from any number of telemarketers, sales reps, and marketing agencies, especially during undesirable times, like the dinner hour. The result of this law is that now companies and sales professionals must ensure that if they are doing B2C calling they must act in compliance with this Federal Law. Additionally, most states now have similar Do-Not-Call registries. This provides another compliance that businesses and sales professionals must adhere to. While there is no such registry for B2B Tele Prospecting calls, sales professionals must still ensure that they are not calling cell phones inappropriately or using a robo-dialer inappropriately, while still honoring the prospect's request to not call if such a request is made.

Despite the huge roadblock that the National DNC places before sales professionals, a large percentage of companies are still using this channel to great benefit. This is due in part to the overall net-benefits that Tele Prospecting affords. However, many prospects who are not any DNC list, have become annoyed by the volume of unexpected phones calls they get from sales professionals. Consequently, these contacts are increasingly refusing to pick up the phone and instead are letting it to go voicemail (and then sometimes blocking the phone number afterward). As such, it is getting difficult (not impossible, but difficult) to reach a prospect via the phones. Remember, before 2007 it took about 3.68 calling attempts to reach a prospect. Today that number is nearly triple. It now takes between eight and twelve calling attempts to reach a prospect. This problem of reaching prospects with fewer call attempts is made worse because of caller ID and the reluctance of gatekeepers to put you through to the prospect.

Making the Phones Work

If you are going to use phones to prospect, and **I highly recommend that you do**, you should know how to do so efficiently and effectively. In my practice, there are generally ten things that we lecture and train our clients on doing to make the best use of Tele Prospecting. These include:

1. Have a targeted list with direct dial numbers
2. Set aside a block of time to dial
3. Know what your call objective is when you call
4. Use a script to achieve that objective
5. Use auto-dialers
6. Leverage Local Presence technology
7. Leave voicemails (VMs)
8. Set call backs
9. Record the calls
10. Know the best time to call

Prospecting in any form is often a tedious and rejection-prone endeavor. Tele Prospecting is no different. Many reps when faced with the reality of prospecting via the phone and the reality of the sheer number of calls needed to reach the RPC (Right Party Contact), get overwhelmed with this task. What reps often attempt to do is eat the buffalo or elephant whole instead of one piece at a time.

Later in this book we will cover the importance of having a targeted list with direct contact information. We will also cover some practical tips on how you can obtain this list. For now, the first step in using Tele Prospecting effectively is to ensure that you have a list of contacts/leads with names and direct phone numbers ready to dial.

Dedicated Block of Time

The second tip is setting aside a block of time each day when you will do your prospecting via the phone. It can be anywhere from two to three hours and could be more or less depending on the calling load and whether you use Tele Prospecting as a mix of strategies or as the sole option. That stated, you want to make sure you close yourself off from distractions, have all the tools you need during the time block and simply get to work. The reason you want to set a block of time for calling is so that you can get into a rhythm. Success with Tele Prospecting is not just about the mechanics of calling, it is also about the level of energy you bring, your focus intensity and your ability to handle rejections and stalls effortlessly. Such a flow only comes about when you can develop a rhythm and move from call to call with minimum breaks in focus.

Call Objective

When you prospect via the phone, like any other channel of contact, you need to know your objective. You must know the answer to this question: *What you are striving to accomplish?* Are you using the phones to identify the RPC? Is this call tasked with setting an appointment with the prospect? Is this call designed to engage in some degree of qualification or gather some additional information? Is this call designed to sell on the phone? What do you want the prospect to do? Whatever your objective, you must be certain that you are clear about it. This is vitally important because knowing your objective helps you assess how effective your calling efforts are. Meaning, did you achieve your objection? Additionally, knowing what your call objective is helps you tremendously in crafting the messages you deliver to the prospect.

The Script

What you say (your message) and how you say it (your delivery) are very important in prospecting. As a matter of fact, scripts are an invaluable part of being effective in all aspects of sales. While scripts can and should be leveraged in just about every communication channel, scripts are especially important when it comes to Tele Prospecting. Keep this in mind; when a potential prospect picks up the phone, you have only a few minutes to pique their interest enough so that they stay on the phone long enough for you to accomplish your objective. (We will cover what to say, and how to say it, when we get to the section on engagement.) Despite their importance, many sales professionals hate the idea of using a script. They believe that if they use a script, they will sound rehearsed. They believe that if they use a script, prospects will know that they are reading lines. Finally, sales professionals fear that by using a script they lose the ability to be creative, adaptable, and spontaneous during the call. While these are valid concerns, they only matter when sales professionals don't master their scripts.

In his book *Way of the Wolf,* Jordan Belfort makes what I think is the strongest case for the use of scripts. He does so by using Hollywood movies as his example.

Every single movie or TV show that made you laugh, cry, shout, or that got you so deeply invested in the characters […] are all scripted. So, if you want to hang onto the false belief that using a script is going to make you sound wooden or inauthentic, […] then you need to ignore the fact that you've spent about half your life being made to laugh and cry and scream and shout as a result of -yes you got it: scripts![2]

So, the real concern should not be rather to use a script or not. NO, the real focus should be on learning how to use scripts effectively, how to write a script and how to master the script so that you don't sound like you are reading from a script. These points ensure that you sound natural, conversational, and creative.

Using an Auto-Dialer

Time is one of the most precious assets that a salesperson has. Therefore, if you must make phone calls, how can you make the best use of your time? One tactic is to automate the calling. In other words, stop manually dialing your calls. Instead, get a business VOIP (Voice Over IP) phone system that has an online portal, or a browser plugin, or some other interface where you can use either a click-to-call system, a power dialing system or preview system. If you are using a CRM (Customer Relationship Management), most have the capacity to integrate a phone system so that when you click a phone number, the number is instantly dialed.

If you don't know which business phone system to use, you can easily use Skype or Google Talk as your "phone system." These two options are relatively easy to use. They both have a browser plugin that, when enabled, grants you the ability to click the phone number in the database record. You can also leverage various other types of virtual contact center software (VCC software) that automates the call, thus saving you tons of time. Why is this important? Because when you reduce wasted time, you optimize contact or connection time.

VCC software also gives you additional ability to integrate other communication software like SMS, emails, and internet-based faxing so that you can have analytics and run reports on how effectively your prospecting activities generate leads.

Lastly, if you do mass prospecting, generally for B2C calls, and you need to get through as many numbers as quickly as possible, then the use of an auto-dialer with the ability to dial multiple phone numbers simultaneously is most definitely the best tool for this job.

Leverage Local Presence

The reality is this, no matter how proficient you become with Tele Prospecting, no matter how targeted your prospecting list, no matter how focused your phone block time, no matter how well you "time" your calls, the majority of calls are still going to go to VMs. Let me repeat, over 51% of the time, the RPC will not immediately pick up the phone. Instead you will get VM. This is just the reality of prospecting by the phone. When that happens, what can, and should, you do?

One option is to leverage technology that increases your pick-up rates. Aside from using auto- dialers, you can also use a phone system that offers "local presence." In its simplest form, local presence is an advance phone system feature which gives the user the ability to automatically dial prospects using local area codes. For example, if your contact is located in New York with an area code of 280, but you are located in Los Angeles with an area code of 310, your "local presence" phone system will automatically display a caller ID with a 280-area code, thus matching the area code of the prospect you are calling. The benefit in using this technology is that if you have direct dial numbers, then you can dramatically increase your pick-up rates or contact rates to be as high as 58%. Moreover, this same local presence phone system has been shown to also increase call back rates by 75%.

Leaving Voicemails (VMs)

To leave a VM or not, that is the question? While "local presence" phone systems will ensure that a significant number of prospects pick up your call, it is not 100%. There will still be a fair number of calls that go to VM. When this happens, many sales professionals ask: *Should I leave a voicemail?* And if yes, *do I leave one every time I call? If I leave a voicemail should I expect a call back?* And finally, *if I leave a voicemail and the prospect does not call me back, was that a waste of time?* There are many experts who differ on their answers to this last question. For example, some experts believe that if you call a list of prospects for whom you have little qualifying information and they don't know you, the probability of a call back from these prospects is low. Thus, leaving a VM, which takes about thirty seconds or more, is an inefficient use of your time. Conversely, there are other experts who argue very forcefully that you should always, always, always leave a VM, every time you call. Who is right?

Auto-Voicemails

The simply answer to the aforementioned question is both. That is both experts are right. If your goal is to get a high rate of call back, then leaving VMs to these prospects is a waste of time. But what if your goal is not to get a call back, but to brand your name, your company, your product? Then doesn't it make sense to leave a VM every time you call? Before deciding, consider a Law of 29 used in Drip Marketing. With this law, a prospect must be exposed to twenty-nine unique messages regarding you, your message, your company, and your offering before familiarity begins. As a matter of fact, this Law of 29 has at its core the Law of Familiarity. According to this Law of Familiarity, it takes a large number of repeated outreaches, repeated exposures to engage a prospect with little to no familiarity with your company. Compared that to one to ten touches to engage an inactive customer, a warm inbound lead or a prospect who already has a high degree of familiarity with you, your company, or your brand. Thus, it does make a lot sense to leave a VM.

As each VM left can take anywhere from thirty seconds or more, if you are leaving a lot of VMs during your call block time, then you might want to consider leaving a pre-recorded voicemail. If you are using an auto-dialer or business VOIP phone system like the one discussed for "local presence" and if that system has an auto-voice mail drop feature, then you can record a general VM that can be used for a calling list where you have little qualifying information about the prospect. This feature will save you time and ensure that you have a high degree of efficiency with your phone-block time. This allows you to leverage every calling opportunity as building brand and company awareness. It also ensures the message is left consistently every time regardless of when you make your outbound calls.

If the prospect, however, represents a potentially high-value deal where you need to leave some personalize information with the goal of incentivizing the prospect to return your call, then leaving a pre-recorded voice-mail will not work. This technique may even send the wrong message that you have not done enough research do find out how your solution can address a very specific need that the prospect might have. The same can be said of prospects with whom you might have had contact with in the past, or where the opportunity is sizable. Thus, leaving pre-recorded VMs for these types of opportunities are counter-productive. With these opportunities, your goal is to get the prospect to return your call, not just brand building. In this spirit, you need to ensure that you are delivering a message that gets you the highest probability of a callback. The way to accomplish that is to leave a structured VM that gives the prospect a reason to call you back. This structure must also make it easy for this prospect to do so.

Structure for Leaving a VM

The structure for leaving a VM is pretty straightforward. It consists of six parts. These include:

1. Mention the contact's first name
2. Identify yourself
3. Say your phone number twice
4. Tell the prospect, the reason for the call
5. Give them a reason to call you back
6. Repeat contact information with phone number a third time

Below is an example of a VM message that I use in my own prospecting efforts. Remember this VM is not for prospects with whom I have already engaged. In those cases, a customized message is left for each opportunity.

> *Hi John (contact's first name). This is Christopher with Bass Christopher & Associates, 818.722.1240, again 818.722.1240. The reason for the call is to schedule a time with you where I may share with you how we help sales teams overcome the biggest challenges to generating qualified prospects and winning the right deals. I did a little research and was curious on a couple things. Give me a call back to discuss. Again, Christopher with Bass Christopher & Associates, 818.722.1240.*

The above VM template is just that, a template. It clearly has all six parts. You can use it to draft your own templates that best fit your business and offerings.

Schedule Call Backs

Depending upon the referred source, the number of call attempts it takes to reach a prospect via the phones varies. The consensus seems to be that before 2007 it took an average of 3.68 attempts to reach a prospect via the phones. Today that number is at least eight to twelve attempts. As such, it is an acceptable part of prospecting for you to make multiple calling attempts if you desire to speak with or get in front of your prospect. Therefore, you should always make it a habit to schedule a call back or schedule a post-activity follow-up. You should do this immediately post activity. Don't wait till the end of the day to schedule the call back. Don't make the mistake of saying that you will get to it later. Schedule the call back now, when it is fresh in your mind.

Record the Calls

Always record your calls. Let me repeat. Always record your calls. This gives you the power to go back and review the calls to ensure that you did not miss any critically important information. It also grants you the ability to QA (qualify assure) the call to know if what you said was on point or if you might have "put your foot in your mouth" or said something stupid. Recording your calls essentially is about knowing unequivocally what is working and what is not working. Now, because different states vary on when and how you can legally record calls, make sure you get legal advice on how best to implement this tip.

Best time to call

When it is the best time to call a prospect? Depending upon the source, the answer to this question is all over the board. Some experts, understandably, argue that the best time to call a prospect is when the prospect has just opened your email. This makes sense if you are using emails as the initial outreach, or if you are using calling and emails as a combo strategy. I recently read a blog post which stated that if you are calling VPs, then any time after 3:00 p.m. is the best time to call. Insidesales.com and Vorsight published a joint research that strongly argues that **the best time to contact a lead is between 8:00 a.m. and 9:00 a.m. or between 4:00 p.m. and 5:00 p.m.**[3] The report also stated the worst time of day to attempt to contact a lead is during lunch hour. As for which days are best, it would seem that the best day of the week to call a prospect is Wednesday and Thursday, while Tuesdays are the worst. They argue that equally important to the best *day* is also the best *time* of day to call. Both points play a critical role in optimizing contact rates. However, a special note must be made, this report collected data based on the first dial.

While I agree there probably is *a best time* to call a prospect, the only way to know for sure with *your prospect* is by calling first, assessing your calling patterns second, and then varying your attempts accordingly. For example, let's say you attempt to reach your prospect by phone with your past three attempts in the morning between 8:00 and 9:00 a.m. Maybe your next call should be sometime in the afternoon. In short, instead of spending so much time analyzing over what is or is not the best time to call your prospect, just call the prospect NOW. From there you should use your results to determine when is the next best time to call.

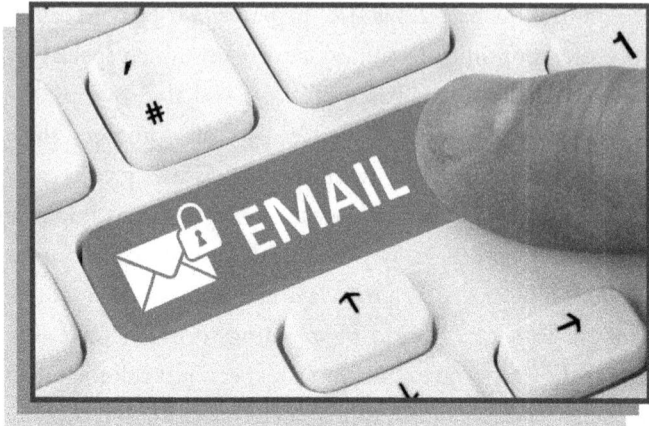

7: Email Prospecting

The mistake people keep making is that if they find a wonderful new tool, like email, they [think they] have to give up all others. They don't. You have simply added another very useful means to your communications repertoire.

– JUDITH MARTIN –

Since the first email system was developed in 1971, book after book, article after article, expert after expert have argued the benefits of using emailing as a prospective tool. Consider these stats:

- Globally there were about 212 billion emails sent daily in 2016. That is according to a report by The Radicati Group Inc[1]
- By the end of 2017 the number of emails sent will be 220 billion and 227 billion by the end of 2018[2]
- Over 205 million emails are sent every second with a mind-blowing number of 74 trillion emails sent yearly
- There are roughly 2.5 billion email users who send these emails[2]

- Eighty-five percent of the world use emails for work and non-work-related matters[3]
- The average business email user sends about forty-one emails a day, while the average consumer sends much less[2]
- The average office worker receives about 121 emails a day[4]
- **Only 34% of all mails are opened[4]**
- The average person deletes 48% of emails they receive daily taking less than five minutes to do so
- Eighty-five percent of professionals name email as their preferred means of business communication[5]
- Fifty percent of salespeople surveyed said they predominantly use emails to communicate throughout the sales process with the client[6]
- **Sixty-five percent of all emails are now opened on mobile devices[7]**

When you account for the fact that some prospects use their social media inbox (like LinkedIn Inbox, Facebook Messengers, Direct Tweets) as a supplement or replacement of the traditional inbox, saying that emails are a valuable tool for prospecting is an understatement. Email has become a central and critical way that we do business and run our lives today. Think about it. An email address is required to sign up for a lot of activities including: social media networking sites, software programs, instant messaging, access to free content, even government agencies ask for your email address when you complete any paperwork.

Thus, the real question is not whether we should or should not use email for prospecting, but rather how should we use Email Prospecting to achieve our prospecting goals? Which is, after all, to get in front of your prospect, evaluate him or her to determine whether you have a qualified lead, so you can move into the selling phase.

Benefits in Using Emails

Emailing in your prospecting effort to contact, engage, and qualify your prospect is a valuable tool. Some sales experts argue that next to Tele Prospecting, Email Prospecting can provide you with the next best Return on Investment (ROI). Email Prospecting can also deliver many more opportunities faster than Social Prospecting. Think about it. Prospecting via email gives you the flexibility to send an email to anyone for whom you can find an email address. Often with the right tool, the finding of the prospect's email is faster and easier compared to finding the prospect's direct dial number.

Secondly emailing allows you to extend your prospecting hours beyond the times you can effectively make phone calls. With the right software like YesWare, Tout, Constant Contact, or any CRM with emailing capability, you can create emails in your downtime and schedule them to go out during the ideal time for when your prospects are mostly likely to see and open them.

Thirdly, Email Prospecting has the added value of being less intrusive and less disruptive than Tele Prospecting. This gives the prospect the luxury to open and read it at his/her own leisure. This means that emailing feels less threatening than Tele Prospecting. No one will hang up on you. Also, you have the opportunity to think about exactly what you want to write before you send it out.

The Challenges with Using Emails

Despite this ubiquitous nature of emailing and the huge benefits it offers, there are some inherent challenges. Because of the sheer amount of emails that prospects receive daily and the amount of time it takes to read each email, prospects scan through their inbox and within three seconds, decide whether to delete your email, read it, or save it for later. This has been called the "Glimpse Factor" by Kendra Lee. With the Glimpse Factor, prospects have three questions top of mind when they first see your email: "1) Do I have time for whatever it is now? 2) Can I delete it and do nothing at all? 3) Do I need to hold on to it to do something later? Because they're busy people, they're secretly hoping that they can delete it with no further action."[7]

As bad as not getting your emails read sounds, there is another challenge to Email Prospecting: not getting your email delivered to the inbox itself. Sometimes this is because of a bad (old or mistyped) email. Other times it's due to being blocked by a spam filter. Also known as an email filter, this is a sophisticated software program that detects unsolicited and unwanted email, and then regulates those emails to a junk or spam folder. These days just about every email client and ISP (Internet Service Providers) use them. Once it's in a spam folder, your emails will die, never to be seen again! So, when you consider these three challenges: 1) Does the prospect even have time to read your email? 2) Will the prospect delete your email and do nothing at all? 3) Will the prospect hold on to your email and read it later? The obvious question for you, the salesperson, becomes: *How can I leverage the power of Email Prospecting to generate sales opportunities for my funnel?*

Tips on Leveraging Email Prospecting

From my experience, there are five things, you must do to ensure that you leverage Email Prospecting effectively:

1. Get the right email address
2. Get your email delivered to the prospects inbox
3. Get your email opened
4. Get your email read
5. Achieve your Email Prospecting objective

Get the Right Email Address

This point will be covered in greater detail in the chapter dealing with finding the contact information for your targeted lists. For now, just know that there are various programs on the market today like RocketReach.co, Rapportive, Mailtester, Toofr, plus a host of others, which can be leveraged to find a prospect's email address. Some of these programs are free, but many of them come with a cost. You can visit the Small Business Ideas Blog[8] for more information. There you will find a published list of over sixty tools you can use to find someone's email address. As of this writing, the URL to this for this blog site is *http://www.smallbusinessideasblog.com/find-email-addresses.* Be mindful that not all of these email-finder programs are created equally, nor are they equally effective. Check out posts on the Beamery Blog[9] or the Sales Handy blog[10] or even Process.st[11] to discover which tool is best for you. Each of these blogs can be found by doing a simple web-search. Once on the blog, find posts on email-finder programs.

Getting the right email address is critical for email delivery. What a waste of time and effort it would be to spend time crafting personalize emails to only have some of them bounce due to bad email addresses. Which, by the way, is one of the ways that ISP and other spam filters use to determine an email sender's reputation. So, having too many bounced emails can cause ISPs to stop allowing your emails into your prospects' inboxes.

Get Your Email Delivered

After obtaining the right email address, or what you believe to be the right email address with a high degree of probability, you will need to ensure your email gets delivered. While I am not an expert on this subject, I do know from personal experience that there are some common-sense tips you can and should use to increase your email deliverability. These include, but are not limited to:

1. Remove bounced email addresses from your database
2. Avoid trigger words that spam filters use to block your emails
3. Avoid images, attachments, videos, and other things that increases the risk of being seen as spammy or that raises red flags

Remove Bounced Email Addresses

Always remove bounced email address from your database. If you are emailing from a CRM such as Salesforce, Zoho, or Sugar, this is easy to do. Once the CRM detects that an email has bounced, the record is automatically flagged, and you are automatically prevented from sending another email to that same bounced email. That email address must be changed if you want to send any subsequent emails to the prospect. If you are not using such a system, then you will have to manually remove that email address from your contact file to ensure that you don't make a mistake later by sending the same bounced email again. Sending bounced emails too many times increases the odds of your email getting caught by the spam filters, thus labeling you a spammer and wham! You might find all your emails getting blocked.

Avoid Trigger Words in Subject Line

HubSpot has a *Free Beginners Guide to Email Marketing.*[12] In this guide, it speaks about how spam filters can be triggered for a variety of reasons. One such reason is using the wrong words or trigger words in your subject line. The guide makes a case that these trigger words are known to cause problems and increase the chances of your email getting caught in a spam trap. But by avoiding these words in your email subject lines, you can dramatically increase your chances of getting past spam filters. The list below, while not exhaustive, gives you an idea of what words to stay away from when you draft your subject line. A more detailed list can be found by Googling this topic.

Email Spam Trigger Words			
This isn't a scam	Earn per week	Mail in order form	Reverses
#1	Easy terms	Maintained	Reverses aging
$$$	Eliminate bad credit	Make $	Risk free
Hidden assets	Eliminate debt	Make money	Rolex
100% free	Email harvest	Marketing	Round the world
100% satisfied	Email marketing	Marketing solutions	S 1618
4U	Expect to earn	Mass email	Safeguard notice
50% off	Explode your business	Medicine	Sale
Accept credit cards	Extra income	Medium	Sales
Acceptance	Free	Meet singles	Sample

Avoid Images, Videos, and Flash

This one I had to learn the hard way. By default, most email clients don't allow the ability to view rich media like Flash or video embeds. Thus, if you do use embedded videos or Flash, you run the risk being blocked by spam filter. What you should do instead is use an image of your video player (with a play button) that links to the rich media on a website page. However, this strategy comes with some risks as well. Many hackers and malware programs use hyperlinks to infect your computer and then steal personal information. Thus, many prospects are highly suspect of links or hyperlinks in the email. So if you put a link in your email make sure you include the full URL description on the link.

Avoid Attachments

If an email has attachments, like images, videos, and hyperlinks, spam filters often block that email. Even if the email gets delivered to the inbox, the filters in the mail client gives the recipient the option of accepting the attachment or not. As most prospects are reluctant to accept attachments from folks they don't know out of the same fear and concerns of hackers stealing information and inserting malware into their computer, you run a very high risk that your valuable, pretty, glossy attachment might never get read.

Avoid Being Flagged by Prospect

The tips above on how to get your email delivered are not exhaustive. If you want to experience the tremendous benefits that Email Prospecting has to offer, then you will need to invest some time in increasing your knowledge and developing the expertise necessary. That stated, you always want to avoid getting flagged as spam by the prospect. Even though you might make it past the guard at the gate (the spam filter) you still have to be accepted by the owner of the house.

To do so, you want to avoid "ALL CAPs" in the subject line. Many experts in Email Prospecting argue that using all caps in the subject line is tantamount or equivalent to yelling at people. Trust me, no one likes to be yelled at, least of all by a stranger and definitely not by a salesperson. A study conducted by the Radicati group found that 85% of respondents prefer an all-lowercase subject line to one in all caps.

Also, don't use exclamation points especially a number of them in a row.

Avoid Non-Company, Impersonal Sender Email Address

Your reply-to address should be a real company email connected to someone human who your subscribers can communicate with. Avoid using an address like *do-not-reply@yourcompany.com*. In fact, you should always use a corporate email account as your sender address. This is a very critical point, because if you use a major ESP and send email using a personal email address such as christopher@yahoo.com or christopher@aol.com, ISPs like Google will block your email. Why? Well, the common understanding is that Yahoo and AOL tell them to! The solution is to use your corporate email address or owned domain.

These tips above are just a start. The goal of this discussion is not to frighten you into never sending an email. On the contrary, the aim is to impress upon you that while prospecting via email can POTENTIALLY be one of the most effective channels for generating qualified sales opportunities, you can also ensure that it ACTUALLY is an effective lead generation channel for yourself. Achieving this, requires you to learn how to leverage this channel effectively.

Get Your Email Opened

Congrats! You succeeded in getting your email delivered. It did not bounce, and it did not get block by the spam filter or the prospect. Mission accomplished, right?

Wrong! So wrong! You still have to ensure that the prospect opens your email. Remember the statistics quoted earlier? The average office worker receives about 121 emails a day, while business executives, get upward of 200+ emails a day especially when you factor in all the social media proxy types inboxes. So again, whether you are the first or the 200th email in the prospects inbox, what can you do to ensure that you get opened?

My own experience augmented with research suggest that there are two things to focus on in getting your email opened by the prospect. These include the email's "from address" and the subject line. As mentioned earlier the "from email" or "senders email" address plays an important role in not just the email's deliverability but also in whether the prospect opens the email. Emails from people that a prospect does not know often don't get opened. Additionally, emails from a generic provider like Gmail or Yahoo, if not immediately deleted, are opened less frequently than emails address with a company domain. So, while it might be tempting to use the Gmail address you have used for years, you can substantially increase your open rates by using a corporate or company-based email address.

Like the "from address," the subject line also plays a role in whether the email is delivered, deleted, or opened. Thus, continuing from the points mentioned above, when looking at the subject line, the prospect asks these questions:

1. Is this for me personally?
2. Is it junk that I can delete or ignore?

Your email subject line should scream "READ ME." It must be relevant to the prospect and pique their interest enough to get them to want to open the email.

Get Your Email Read

OK, your email was delivered, and it was opened. Congrats, you have achieved a success rate that only 30% of the emailers achieved. But how do you know if your email had been read in its entirety? The easy answer to this question is to see if the prospect took the next step and performed your call-to-action (CTA). Maybe that CTA was to click on a link? Maybe that CTA was to fill out a form?

Maybe that CTA was to schedule a time to speak directly on your calendar? Or maybe it was simply to respond to your email? Whatever the particular CTA is, if that is done by the prospect then you will know that the email was read. But is there another way to determine if the email was read without the prospect performing the CTA. **Reportedly only 3.2% of emails opened have a click-through rate**. But that does not mean that the email was not read. There are a couple of things that you can do to increase the likelihood that your emails are read once opened.

Believe it or not, but the opening "Salutation" plays a critical role here. Emails that are not addressed specifically to the prospect, meaning not using the prospect's name, are typically not read, and often deleted. This is because if it does not use the prospect's name, the prospect assumes, rightly or wrongly, that it was not intended for him or her.

Additionally, the length and format of the body of the email determines if your email will be read. Prospects with so many things to do and so many other emails to go through, don't have the time to read a long email from someone they don't know. Also, remember that **75% of all emails are opened on mobile devices**. Thus, the body of the email must be optimized and small enough to read in its entirety on a mobile device. You must keep the length of the body concise and to the point.

I am often asked this question: *If I do all the above, am I guaranteed to get my email delivered, opened, read, and converted?* The reality is no. There are no guarantees other than if you don't do these things you have no chance of getting in front of that prospect via email. What you can do, however, is use the above tips WITH some form of email tracking software to track the degree to which you are successful. Remember, to leverage Email Prospecting effectively, you want to know:

1. Was my email delivered or bounced?
2. Was my email opened? If so, how many times? At what times? On what device?
3. Was my emailed forwarded?
4. Were any links clicked?
5. Was my email read in its entirety?

Programs like Yesware, Tout, Mailchimp, and Constant Contact provide you with answers to these questions so that you can make intelligent decisions about what is and is not working with your Email Prospecting.

8: SMS Prospecting

The poem is a form of texting...it's the original text.
It's a perfecting of a feeling in a language – it's a way of
saying more with less, much as texting is.

– CAROL ANN DUFFY –

It should come as no surprise that texting or SMS messaging is a hot thing now. While texting has been around since the 1980s, businesses and sales professionals have only recently begun to leverage SMS messaging's potential in marketing, sales, and service. SMS messages are being used for things like following up with prospects who downloaded a white paper, or a salesperson confirming and reminding a prospect of an appointment, or the service team sending account related information to the prospects. Business of all sizes from all industries are leveraging the power of this promising prospecting tool with a very high ROI potential.

I can relate my own experience here. Having purchased a ticket to fly from LAX to Romania and back during Christmas 2017, I immediately got (post purchase), a text thanking me for my purchase and providing me with flight information with links to check and modify my flight plans. Moreover, every change or modification to my flight plan resulted in me getting subsequent SMS updates. There were even clickable links in the SMS message where I could login into my account online and see the details.

Consider the following. There are an estimated 4.77 billion mobile phones used around the world.[1] Of this number, 75% of all phones are texted enabled.[2] There were approximately 8.3 trillion text messages sent in 2017.[3] This means that 23 billion SMS messages are sent daily, resulting in 16 million texts being sent every minute. Not surprisingly, **SMS messages have an open-rate of 98%.**[4] WOW! Now compare these numbers to emailing, which has on its best days an open rate of 22%.[5] The average person spends about 23 hours a week texting.[6] Over one third of business professionals say they can't go ten minutes without responding to a text.[7] Ninety percent of texts are read within three to five minutes of receipt.[8] **Text messages have a 45% response rate while emailing has just 6%.**[9]

I know, mind blowing, right?

Benefit of Using SMS for Prospecting

If you Googled the question, "What are the top five benefits of using SMS as a prospecting tool?" You might come back with 1.2 million returns. One search result that caught my eye was one by SimplyCast. Being a business communication automation company with offices in North America, Australia, and the UK, SimplyCast published a blog post entitled "The TOP 10 Benefits of SMS Marketing" (prospecting).[10] Their list includes:

1. Instant Deliverability
2. Flexible Platform
3. Instant Opt-In and Opt-Out
4. High Open Rate
5. High Conversion Rate
6. Reliable
7. Short Messages;
8. Cool Factor
9. Limitless Marketing Potential
10. Green

There are many experts, books, and articles that would probably list many more. Here, I am going to discuss just one of which you should be mindful.

My own experience suggests that prospects who receive SMS messages during the any part of the sales process **convert a high rate over those who do not receive any such messages**. As a matter of fact, Smart Insights reports that sending a simple follow-up message, "Have you read our email?" to people who opted-in for that type of SMS increased conversion by 20% to 30%.[11] Other SMS platform providers say that SMS Prospecting, when done effectively and efficiently, increases contact rates, drives relevant conversations with your prospect, nurtures the prospect with relevant content and engagement, shorten the sales cycle, and ultimately increases sales conversions.

Issues with Using SMS Prospecting

With so much upside, there is, unfortunately, a dark side to SMS Prospecting. Compared to face-to-face and telephone communications, texting is a highly impersonal communication tool. Yet, because we treat our SMS inbox as sacred and only allowing for family, friends, and close associates text us, we treat texting like we do face-to-face and voice communication. Consequently, there are a number of consumers who simply do not want to ever get solicitations from a salesperson. Period. If a company or salesperson is not carefully in how they seek to leverage that power of SMS Prospecting, they run huge risk.

Companies that fail to leverage SMS messaging properly (for example, legally and responsibly) also run the risk of incurring huge fines. You might not have read about the case involving Heartland Automotive Services, the largest Jiffy Lube franchise in America. In 2012, Heartland Automotive Services and TextMarks settled a lawsuit for $47 million. They were alleged to have illegally sent SMS messages to 2.3 million mobile numbers. According to an article written by Tatango[12] (a competitor of TextMarks), while that $47M settlement may sound large, it could have been much, much worse. The TCPA sets statutory damages in the amount of $500 per violation. Meaning that the total penalty/fine levied against Heartland and TextMarks could have amounted to $1.15 *billion* in damages. To add insult to injury, a court could rule that if your business willfully or knowingly violates the TCPA, the court could triple the amount of damages, which means a business could be sued for up to $1,500 per text message!

Get Opt-In Permission

Before jumping into the details of how you can use SMS effectively, I want to address the 800-pound gorilla in the room. That is, the legal side of using SMS. Now, I am not an attorney, yet it would be remiss of me not to mention the Opt-In requirement for SMS message compliance. I will speak briefly about a case I read on the Tatango website. By the way, Tatango is a SMS marketing company founded in 2007 and based out of Seattle, Washington. The company is purported to have a number of industry-leading awards and when you consider its portfolio of clients, it is hard to argue that Tatango does not come with some degree of gravitas to this conversation. That stated, the company published an article entitled "Can I Text Message My Customers Legally?"[13] The blog posts go on to explain what you need to do when you are collecting your customers' mobile phone numbers. Accordingly, you must disclose the following two things to them in a "clear and conspicuous" manner. If you are wondering like I was what the heck this meant, well, it means that the disclosures must be displayed in close proximity to wherever you were when you asked customers for their mobile phone numbers.

The two disclosures are:

1. By participating, you consent to receive text messages sent by an automatic telephone dialing system, and

2. Consent to these terms is not a condition of purchase

Failure to disclose the above in a "clear and conspicuous" manner, will put you in direct violation. If caught, it could cost you anywhere from $500 to $1,500 per text message violations.

And there you have it. Again, let me repeat I am not an attorney, but if you are going to use SMS as prospecting tool, then I highly advise you to seek the advice of your legal counsel to determine what your options and risks are as you weigh the insanely great ROI that SMS can and does bring to the table.

When to Use SMS

It would seem in many cases that texting in business context is an earned privilege. If you want to avoid the possibilities of fines like the Jiffy Lube case, then using SMS for the initial outreach is a risky strategy. Most experts strongly advise to never use SMS as the initial outreach unless other contact channels have proven unsuccessful. For the past five years or so, I have used SMS as an initial outreach to outbound generated leads ONLY as means of last resort. In particular with buyer-initiated leads and with outbound leads with whom I have had prior contact. In other words, I do use texting as part of a larger contact strategy. Generally, I use it as a means of getting additional information, staying engaged with the prospect, providing value by sending reference materials that are relevant to my prospect's unique needs and challenges, or simply to confirm next steps.

However, if my other attempts, calling, emailing, inmails, direct mail, In-Person Prospecting efforts have proven unsuccessful, and I have the RPC's cell phone number, then I will use that as part of my attempt to get in contact with the RPC. I only leverage it as a one-to-one effort and never with mass texting. I figured that if I have not been successful at this point and I have exhausted every other means what do I have to lose by leveraging SMS in this way. Remember, however, that this is the strategy that I use as one of last resort.

Other Times to Use SMS for Prospecting

According to Velocify, prospects who receive SMS messages "during the sales process" **convert at a rate 40% higher than those who do not receive such messages**. While the research found the companies were sending these SMS messages both before contact and post contact, messages sent after contact via the phone improved conversions by 112.6%. This is compared to just 4.8% below the average for messages sent pre-contact. During these post contact times, salespeople can keep prospects engaged and reduce the sales cycle time by sending relevant, information, appointment confirmation, and appointment reminders. SMS can also be used to send information that requires an immediate response

How Should You Use It?

Always identify yourself in the message using "First and Last Name" and "Name of Company." Also, you want to make sure you keep your messages short and to the point. Because this is not a personal outreach, resist the urge to treat it like an SMS to your buddies. In other words, remember the tone of your SMS message. Watch for grammar issues. Do not use abbreviations like LOL, or BFF of JK in your text body. You should be friendly, polite, and easy going, but still professional.

How Many Text Messages Should You Send?

With the "What to send?" and "When to send?" questions answered, the next question that I get asked frequently is, "How many text messages should I send a prospect?" I also get "How many is too many?" and "How many is not enough?"

The simple answer is don't over-text your prospect. I realize this might be an oversimplification of the question. Therefore, why don't we consider a study conducted by Velocify and written by Nick Hedges. In this study, Velocify's research strongly suggests that salespeople "[...] should send as many SMS messages as the interaction [...] requires."[13] That is because more texts equate to greater engagement, and thus a higher rate of conversation. They argue that three or more purposeful texts after contact can increase conversion rates by 328%.

SMS Messaging Software for Business

Before ending this discussion on leveraging SMS messaging as the third leg of a comprehensive prospecting strategy, I want to briefly touch upon the technology side. In order to know what works, what does not work, and how SMS message impacts the lead generation and prospecting efforts, I highly advise that you use business SMS messaging software. Additionally, you should use this software as an integrated part of your CRM.

There are a number of business SMS messaging platforms. If you conducted a Google search you might get a return of 5.3 million hits.

This would include companies like Trumpia, Ex Texting, CallRail, TextUs, and Sendhub, just to name a few. All of these are platforms give the user the ability to:

1. Manage inbound and outbound SMS messaging to individuals or groups
2. Provide telephone numbers, business lines and shortcodes, CRM integration, analytics and reporting, plus a host of other cool features

These systems are critical to optimizing the efficiency and maximing the effectiveness of your SMS Prospecting efforts. These platforms also provide you with the necessary tools, resources, and expertise to be and stay compliant with TCPA laws governing responsible and legal uses of SMS messaging for business.

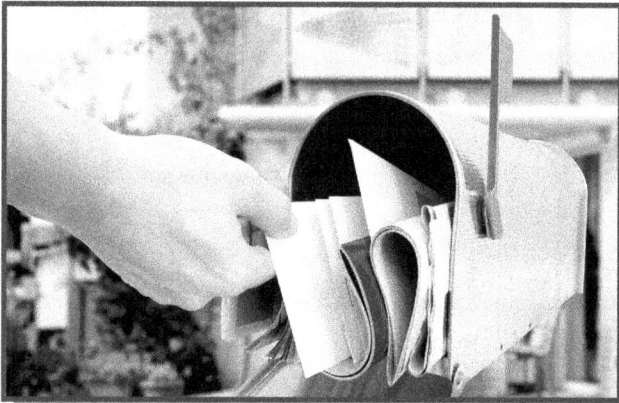

9: Direct Mail Prospecting

I love the rebelliousness of snail mail, and I love anything that can arrive with a postage stamp. There's something about that person's breath and hands on that letter.

– DIANE LANE –

According to the DMA (Data & Marketing Association), 9.8 billion catalogs were mailed in 2016. From these, 100.7 million U.S. adults made a catalog purchase in 2016.[1] Some might think that in the age of the email, that direct mail is dead. To think so would be short-sighted, because there are a number of industries and businesses that still use direct mail for generating prospects, winning new clients, and servicing clients as well. Whether you agree with the aforementioned numbers or not, the ultimate question to ask is does using direct mail for prospecting make any sense in the world of emails, SMS messages, and the Social Selling 2.0 crazy? Does it make sense to take the time and send personalized mail to the prospect?

From my own results (remember I prospect daily for new opportunities) and the results of my clients, the answer is *yes*. Yes, it does make sense. Additionally, I have spoken with countless other sales professionals with whom

I network and heard them recount situation after situation when a well-crafted and well timely letter opened the door to a qualifying conversation with an otherwise difficult to reach prospect. In essence, there are still many benefits to using direct mail with your lead generation efforts, but to do so, you must find ways of overcoming the top challenges with this method.

Benefits of Direct Mail Prospecting

In an article written by Steve Slaunwhite, a business author, copywriter, and speaker on copying and freelancing, he states that one of the greatest benefits to direct mail is that it tends to stand out more so than ever before.[2] This is true because in the crowded digital world of emailing and social media it's increasingly harder to stand out.

Remember from our discussion on Email Prospecting, the average prospect gets anywhere from 141-200 emails daily compared to the **average prospects getting less than forty mail pieces a day**. Plus, it is much easier to get the correct address of the prospect as compared to the getting the correct email address. You can verify an address is correct before sending a piece of mail, but you can't verify an email address without sending the email.

Also, direct mail has a higher response rate than email. According to a report by DMA (Data & Marketing Association), 79% of direct mail consumers respond immediately to direct mail advertisement while only 45% of email receipts do the same.[3] The DMN3 reported that 39% of consumers first patronize a business because they received a direct mail advertisement.[4] Consequently, Ms. Prospect is more likely to notice your snail mail before your email. This is even greater when the direct mail piece is handwritten and the envelope hand addressed.

Challenges in Direct Mail Prospecting

The number one challenge with Direct Mail Prospecting rests in getting your mail in the hands of your intended audience. If your target has a gatekeeper, then this deliverability is even more difficult, because often your direct mail might get stopped by that gatekeeper. While some say statistically, the deliverability of direct mail is better than email, you still have to hope the mail piece gets delivered.

Additionally, it is more time consuming to send a direct mail piece. Rather it is the crafting of the letter, selecting the proper stationary, addressing the envelope, getting postage, and mailing. Then you have to wait days for it to be delivered. Not knowing if it was delivered. You hope that it *does* get delivered. Unless you take the extra step of sending it certified mail.

Finally, there is the challenge of cost. Other than In-Person Prospecting, Direct Mail Prospecting tends to be much more expensive than any other type. Because of these factors, direct mail tends to take a back seat to other less expensive options.

Five Types of Direct Mail

There are generally five types of direct-mail-based on formats:

- Postcards
- Self-mailers
- Letters
- Dimensional mailers
- Catalogs

Each direct mail piece has purpose and benefits. Postcards are said to be the cheapest and simplest of all direct mail pieces to send. They tend to work better for customers rather than prospects. Self-mailers are brochures that fold into themselves and stay shut with an adhesive tab. These are great for prospecting as they can give the prospect a broad picture of the company. They also tend to be a lot more expensive than post-cards. Letters are great for confidentiality or when sensitive data is being delivered. These really work well for high-level prospecting and are best when personalized. Dimensional mailers look fresh and upscale. They are often used for high-level business contacts when you want to bypass the mailroom and the human gatekeeper. Finally, catalogs showcase a wide range of products. These tend to be the most expensive of all direct mail pieces. They can be as simple as three to five pages to highly complex, glossy, elaborate booklets. They are most often use for current customers particularly in cross selling or upselling opportunities. But they can be leveraged for high level prospects as well.

Practical Steps for Using Direct Mail

Considering the above-mentioned benefits in light of the challenges, what follows are practical steps that you can take to leverage the power of Direct Mail for your prospecting efforts. Be mindful, that from a prospecting standpoint, the usages of direct mail are limited, in my opinion. Yet it is usable in certain cases. Below are my six quick tips.

1. **Avoid teaser copy.** Anything with FREE, Urgent, Special Offer or anything of the sort will not make it past the mailroom and if it does, it will not get past the gatekeeper because it screams junk mail.

2. **Use dimensional mail.** According to Ernest Nicastro, author of *Making it Past White Fang: How to Reach Senior Level Executives with Direct Mail*, dimensional mail is anything that is uniquely packaged. I am speaking about any envelope of various sizes, or anything mailed in a box. These typically make it past the mailroom.

3. **Send certified mail to ensure delivery.** Not only does certified mail get past the mailroom and the gatekeeper but it also looks official. Sending it certified creates a sense of urgency. Additionally, it's traceable given that the recipient (or someone on their behalf) must sign for it.

4. **Write professionally.** When drafting an actual letter, follow the same tips on how to write emails that get opened and get read.

5. **Provide value.** Always, always, always offer something of value or something from which the prospect can benefit.

6. **Encourage a call to action (CTA).** Give the prospect a compelling reason to give you a call, write back, or at the very least accept your call the next time.

These tips are not intended to be exhaustive. No. These few tips are designed to help you get your strategically designed direct mail piece delivered, opened and read by the intended prospect. If you want to leverage Direct Mail in a larger context, I recommend you read Craig Simpson's book entitled, *The Direct Mail Solution: A Business Owner's Guide to Building a Lead-Generating, Sales Driving, Money Making Direct-Mail Campaign.*[5]

10: Fax Prospecting

*A value is like a fax machine; it's not much use
if you're the only one who has one.*

– KWAME ANTHONY APPIAH –

Before there was email, just about every business used the fax machine for many things, including prospecting. Yes, I know, hard to believe. Nonetheless, with the dominance of email as a preferred method for written prospecting, where does this leave the fax machine? Has the fax machine just gone the way of the dinosaur or the fanny pack? Or is the fax machine, like the wrist watch, something we buy simply because we feel we must have one, yet we rarely use it?

Before answering these questions, let take a brief look back at the history of the fax machine.

The fax machine has its origin in the mid-1800s when Alexander Bain invented the first technology to send an image over a wire. Over the years, various inventors from Frederick Bakewell, to Giovanni Caselli, to Richard H. Ranger made modifications and advanced the technology. Effectively, these additions and modifications produced what we know now as the modern-day fax machine. The technology was so widespread and used as the principal means of doing business around the world that it became the first truly universal method for secure global communications.

All that however changed in the first decade of the twenty-first century when we saw major growth in the functions of the Internet replacing the everyday fax machine.[1] While many businesses still rely upon the fax machine for secure, reliable communications, especially when signatures are needed in realtime,[2] online faxing or Internet-based faxing has taken over as it merges the function of the fax with the convenience of the Internet. Despite this decline, there are still a lot of organizations that rely heavily on faxing. There are some businesses and governmental agencies that still send volumes of faxes daily.

Use of the Fax Machine

Faxes are still used to quickly send and receive documents that require a signature. This reception is obtained faster than direct mail or hand delivered mail. And yes, while e-signing programs like DocuSign and HelloSign exist, some businesses and customers distrust the electronic signatures in favor of the hardcopy, handwritten signatures. While working as a Director of Sales for a telcom company, the universal understanding in the firm (maybe even the industry) was that, in remote areas where the Internet is slow or non-existent, a fax machine hooked up to a phone line is still the main source of communications when it comes to lengthy orders, messages, and sharing other information. When you think about it, in these types of situations, fax machines work well especially in sending emergency communications and the status of account and delivery information.

Patrick Phelps, in his article entitled "Uses of Faxes in Business," says that using fax machines to prospect is still an effective method for some companies[3] He lists examples like a restaurant sending out daily specials to local businesses or an equipment dealer sending out exciting promotions. That stated, is faxing effective for prospecting?

While I don't use faxing heavily for prospecting, I do know of a number of sales professionals, primarily in real estate or the timeshare industry, who *do* use faxes religiously in their prospecting efforts. These tend to be more broadcast faxes as opposed to one-to-one faxing. I have often heard these reps boldly claim that without their trusted fax machines they would not have closed as much business as they had over their sales' career.

Benefits of Using Faxes

Depending on the source, the benefits of using faxes vary. Some say that it is faster than direct mail, and you can get a hard, handwritten signature faster than by way of an electronic signature. Secondly, as long as the fax number is correct, delivery is 100% guaranteed. With the email inbox clutter and voicemails not being returned, a fax message sent directly to the end-user's fax machine (assuming that it is a hardline and not email based) will automatically be delivered without the prospect needing to accept it. Thirdly, the fax machine is attached to a hard phone line, which is the most secure communication channel. And lastly, a fax is less expensive to send than Direct Mail, In-Person, or Tele Prospecting.

Challenges with Using Fax Prospecting

The biggest problem with a traditional fax machine is that it interrupts your workflow. It takes you away from your workstation and inevitably involves you with other issues on the way to or from the fax machine.[4] Granted, this challenge will have less of an impact as more users migrate to email-based faxing or online fax services. Additionally, unless the receiver has his or her own fax machine, faxes are usually printed out in an area shared by other employees, and thus not conducive for confidential information. Unlike an email, as long as you have the right email address (you just have to be concerned with getting past the spam filters), fax prospecting requires the receiver's fax machine be turned on and that the machine is not out of paper. Both of which can delay significantly the delivery and the viewing of the fax message.[5] And while email can send voice files, video clips, links, and high-resolution photographs, a fax machine can send only paper documents.

Do these challenges make it seem like using fax prospecting is not as great of a tool after all? Remember, that all four challenges can be eliminated if instead of using a hard fax machine in this process, you use a fax-to-email service. Problem resolved! This alternative, however, is subject to the same challenges as emails, because it uses emailing as the method of delivery,

Tips for Leveraging Fax Prospecting

If you use faxing as a prospecting tool, there are some best practices to consider.

1. **The Law.** Become familiar with the unsolicited-fax laws of the states you are sending the faxes to. Penalties for sending unsolicited faxes are set at $500 in statutory damages for each violation and/or any actual monetary losses, whichever is greater.[6]

2. **Limit your fax to one page.** When sending faxes, it is best to keep your message short regardless of the type of fax (flyer, newsletter, update, or announcement). Prospects don't have time to read lengthy promotional messages. **Remember you are competing for the prospect's attention which is already very limited.** Just like other forms of written communications, you have a few seconds to capture the attention of the reader before they decide to trash your fax. Keep the fax transmission simple and limited to just one page. Don't flood your prospect with mounds of paper.

3. **Have a clean subject line.** Similar to email, you want to ensure that your subject line does not include terms that normally throw up red flags – terms like, FREE; Hidden Secrets; Risk FREE; This isn't a scam; Foolproof. Remember, the subject line should scream "READ ME." It must be relevant to the prospect and pique enough interest to get the prospect to *want* to read your fax.

4. **Provide a strong call to action.** Like email, what is it that you want your prospect to do once they read the fax? This is your call-to-action (CTA). Maybe that CTA is to give you a call? Maybe the CTA is to visit your website? Maybe it is to schedule a time to speak directly? Maybe it is to take advantage of a particular offer? Whatever it is, make sure that it is clearly stated, direct, and has no strings attached. Otherwise your prospect will treat your fax like a scam and toss it in the trash.

5. **Provide a signature.** Always include your company's name, contact information, and website in a signature. If you have social media profiles, include those as well. The aim is to show the prospect that you are a legitimate company, and that there are places for them to find additional information about you and your company.

6. **Give an opt-out option.** When sending faxes, give recipients a way to opt-out of receiving any further faxes. You can do so by either placing a line or two of text at the bottom of every fax page to let recipients know how they can opt out or you can include a toll-free number for them to call or fax.

While I don't use Fax Prospecting all that frequently, I have used it selectively when no other means of contacting the prospect has worked and when I do have a direct fax number to the prospect. When you think about today's climate, when other prospecting channels are becoming exceedingly crowded, leveraging Fax Prospecting could pay huge dividends by cutting through the noise and standing out.

11: In-Person Prospecting

Obstacles are necessary for success because in selling,
as in all careers of importance, victory comes only after
many struggles and countless defeats.

– OG MANDINO –

In-Person Prospecting, also known as field canvassing or door-to-door marketing, is a prospecting channel that attempts to use face-to-face visits as the vehicle for getting into immediate contact with the RPC. In-Person Prospecting and Tele Prospecting are the only two prospecting channel options that can obtain immediate and direct interaction with the potential prospect. Believe me when I say this, door-to-door prospecting is probably one of the hardest and most despised types of prospecting by sales professional and prospects alike. Nevertheless, In-Person Prospecting can and does work well for both B2B and B2C situations where the products lend themselves to consultation or demonstration. Lead Heroes wrote *The Complete Guide to Door-To-Door Cold Knocking*. It states In-Person Prospecting works well for product that rely on detailed explanations regarding how the offering differs from that of competitors or to provide instruction – the one-on-one interaction afforded by door-to-door sales gives this approach an advantage over the store environment.[1]

Due to the amount of time it consumes, many businesses and salespersons have severely limited the amount time they spend doing In-Person Prospecting. Some have eliminated it altogether and replaced it with other in-office type of prospecting (Tele Prospecting, Email Prospecting, Social Prospecting). However, there are businesses like real estate, insurance, solar, food delivery, magazine subscriptions, and Internet services, in which In-Person Prospecting is on the rise. With the advent of the National DNC registry, and state No-Call List, Tele Prospecting is no longer (as viable) of an option for real estate personnel to find a new customer. Consider these numbers from Robert Hartline of CallProof.com, In-Person Prospecting is a growing segment for direct selling. From 2013 to 2014 U.S., retail sales in the direct selling channel increased 5.5%, bringing in an estimated $34.47 billion, an industry record high.[2] You may try to dismiss this tactic as dated and ineffective, but the fact remains that this **$34 billion industry is still on the rise.**

Benefits of In-Person Prospecting

Because of the National DNC and State No-Call List, it is getting harder and harder to get into direct contact with buyers via the phone for certain industries. For companies like solar, insurance, and real estate, In-Person Prospecting is the only valid option. Secondly, going door-to-door, gives you the invaluable opportunity to get some additional intel by allowing you to talk to people who are not the RPC. You can speak with gatekeepers, security guards, and other possible influencers in the selection and purchase of certain products/services for the business. You might even be able to gain some much-needed intel on who the incumbent vendor is and if there are any known issues that end users face or deal with on a day-to-day basis. Thirdly, visiting a prospect in person, gives you access to clues that you would never have a chance to uncover over the phone. Clues like hobbies, office set up, what the prospect has hanging on his or her walls, the style of dress, demeanor, and body language. Finally, visiting in-person gives you the opportunity to get in to see a buyer who might be hard to reach by phone because if you time it correctly, you might be able to catch the person coming into work, leaving for lunch, or going home for the day.

Issues with In-Person Prospecting

One of the major issues with In-Person Prospecting is in-person rejection. A fair number of sales professionals can easily weather rejection over the phone, but find it crushingly devastating to get rejected in person. The second issue with In-Person Prospecting is that it takes up a lot of time. This is true whether the In-Person drop-in visits are structured or unstructured. Next to Fax Prospecting, In-Person Prospecting in probably the least efficient in terms of time management. Disagree? Consider these factors: it takes you more time to get to the location; it takes you longer to get to see the RPC; if you are unsuccessful in getting in to see the intended contact, then you spend a lot of time traveling back to the office. True, you can make good use of the travel time to and from the locations by making calls to other prospects while in the car and maybe you have other places to visit nearby. However, this investment of time often leaves you empty-handed.

Despite its time cost, In-Person Prospecting is most definitely one of the best, next to Tele Prospecting, in terms of effectiveness. This is because once you do get in front of the RPC, you can use a lot of verbal and non-verbal (tonality and body language) techniques to engage and qualify the prospect, bond and build rapport, develop a relationship, and move the call to the next step.

Considering both the pros and cons of In-Person Prospecting, you might be wondering when is it best to leverage In-Person Prospecting? The answers are when you need to:

1. Identify the RPC
2. Gather more intel on the company, the RPC, and its competitors
3. Determine if the business is or should be a potential target
4. Nurture and build a relationship
5. Get in contact with the RPC or the main influencers, if they are hard to reach by phone.

Tips on Leveraging In-Person Prospecting

To increase the effectiveness and efficiency of In-Person Prospecting, there are some steps that you should follow to make this prospecting channel both effective and efficient.

1. **Be Flexible**. Unless other prospecting channels are closed to you, like Tele Prospecting for some B2C professionals, then you should always attempt to use In-Person Prospecting as a supplement or complement to other forms of prospecting.

2. **Be Focused**. Because In-Person Prospecting can be a big-time waster, never take a random approach. Always make your visits strategic and as part of a larger field-prospecting day.

3. **Make a Schedule**. If you can, schedule an appointment with an existing prospect or an existing customer in the same area as your intended contact. You can make this easier by looking for other leads that you either have not had success in contacting by the phone or email, or where you have lost contact with the RPC. If you are unable to set an appointment with any surrounding leads, visit the intended contact anyway.

4. **Use the T-Call Approach**. After your scheduled in-person visits, use the T-Call Approach to find other possible businesses that might be a good target. The T-Call Approach is when you are at the existing prospect's place, and you look to the right of you, to the left of you, and behind you for other possible opportunities. If any of these new suspects are found, then you should at least do a drop-in and gather as much intel as you can.

5. **Use Your CRM**. If you have a CRM and a mobile app version of it, use it. Let me say it again, use it. Meaning use it to search for existing leads and do drop-ins on those leads. Presently, I use Zoho CRM with its mobile app. I have a feature that allows me to click on a map and search for leads, contacts, or accounts that are near my present location. Of course, the app knows my present location because I have the location finder enabled on my phone.

6. **Get Past Building Security**. This one is hard to do. While I have read a number of techniques that range from lying to the security to pretending to be a tenant in the building, the only methods that I have found to work is asking for help. You should always be upfront with why you are there and get the security to offer suggestions on how best to get up to see the intended contact. Surprisingly, this has worked more often than not. Does it work every time? Of course not.

What it does, is help you establish a degree of credibility with the security, so that if you can't get through this time, at least you have a better chance next time. Often on the third or fourth visits, you should have built enough goodwill with the security guard that your chances get increasingly better to get in.

7. **Rely on Gatekeepers**. Learn how to effectively use the gatekeeper to get you in to see the RPC, either at that very moment or later (get on the RPC's calendar). Just like Tele Prospecting, never be confrontational. Always treat the gatekeepers with respect. Don't lie or give false information. Always seek to find ways to get the gatekeeper on your side.

8. **Know Your Goal**. When you are successful in getting in front of the RPC, make sure you know exactly what you are there for, be prepared to follow your strategy, and achieve it quickly.

9. **Be Prepared to Perform**. Lastly, when the prospect gives you time, be ready to demonstrate how you can help. You need to be prepared at all times to present on the spot. This is true even for less complicated products, but only if your product lends itself to impromptu presentations.

12: Net Prospecting

The richest people in the world look for and build networks, everyone else looks for work.

– ROBERT KIYOSAKI –

You are probably very familiar with the person whose goes to networking events with the sole purpose of handing out as many business cards he can while also collecting the same number in return. He may or may not attempt to make a meaningful connection. He may not begin to develop a relationship. His goal may simply be to get his business cards out to as many people as he can. In this sense, he is using the networking event not for building relationships, but rather as a promotion opportunity. Meaning, he is using the event as a means to get exposure and attention. And of course, that is not a bad strategy.

Contrastingly, maybe you have seen the networker who seems to be great with people. She has a fun way of introducing herself and then getting the other person to share details, sometimes intimate details about themselves and their businesses. She knows how to work the room, and she seems very well-known. She gets a few referrals a month from contacts she meets at these events based on the force of her personality and charisma, but because she never follows up with 90% of the people she met, her results are a shadow of what they should be.

And then there's the guy who shows up because his boss told him to. Or how about the business professional that knows (based on his research) that networking is the best method of building his sales pipeline. Yet he is too painfully shy to approach anyone. However, as soon as a stranger approaches him and introduces himself, the previously-shy business professional begins to talk the person's ear off, literally telling this poor person his entire life story?

Are any of these scenarios networking? Are they networking effectively? Granted, if any of these people knew better, they would take the contact information obtained during these events and add this information to their trusted CRM, making sure to also include any other pertinent information discussed. These networkers would also began making follow-up calls to each new contact, hopefully to those with whom he might have pre-qualified as a potential or strategic contact. Maybe even setting up a few in-person appointments to accomplish the same objectives.

If all of these things were done, would you answer the aforementioned two questions differently? If you were to ask either Bob Burg, author of *Endless Referrals 3rd Edition*,[1] or Ivan Misner, founder of BNI (Business Networking Inc) and author of *Networking Like a Pro*,[2] they would both say no. Meaning, that none of the networkers mentioned above are networking the right way or networking effectively.

Defining Networks and Networking

If you Googled "definition of network" you might find these definitions among the results.

1. Network is an arrangement of intersecting horizontal and vertical lines. Like a complex system of roads, railroads, or other transportation routes.

2. Network is a group or system of interconnected people or things. This might include a group of people who exchange information, contacts, and experience for professional or social purposes.

Taking the second definition, an easy way of defining network is that it's a collection or the sum total of all contacts you know. With this collection of intra-relational contacts, there are many objectives that the networker can set to achieve. And while this definition is not meant to be all-inclusive in scope, it is meant to serve as a starting point for our discussion on what I refer to as Net Prospecting. Meaning, networking for the sole purpose of generating qualified sales opportunities for your pipeline.

If you were to ask most sales professionals to define network, I am certain that most might say that a network is a collection of known contacts (personal or business) that are connected to each other based on a number of different relationships and roles. For example, when you consider the contacts in your network, whom do you have? You might have family and friends of course. You might have roommates. You might have members from a particular team on which you play or had played. You might have current and ex-significant others. You might have co-workers, direct reports, and superiors. You might have teachers whose classes you took. You might have doctors, lawyers, or politicians. The list of possible people in your network is immense. Unless however, you agreed with Joe Girard, the current Guinness Book of World Record holder for having sold 13,001 cards in fifteen years. In his book *"How to Sell Anything to Anybody"* Joe states that each of us have a personal sphere of influence of about 250 people. He refers to this as Girard's Law of 250.[3]

Regardless of the source, I am confident that most networking experts generally define networking as the act of developing, growing, and leveraging the contacts in your sphere of influence for a number of different reasons. Networking can be used for both business and personal reasons.

For example, you may be new to an area and would like to network to develop some friends. Or you might be a recent college grad and thus networking to find a new career. Alternatively, you may even be a seasoned vet but still looking to connect with people who could help you advance your career. You may be an entrepreneur with a great business idea but still need capital to fund the business, thus you might be networking to find and connect with investors. Or you might be a sales professional looking for additional means of filling your pipeline with prospects and thus you are looking to connect to get some referrals. Hopefully it is clear by now that the reasons for networking are limited only by our own imagination. If so, great. Now let's continue this discussion.

Networking of any kind is not simply an information exchange between you and another person. It is significantly more than that. When you think about it, most experts and sales professionals see business networking as leveraging business and personal connections to bring in a regular supply of new business. While this is so true, the only slight change I would make to this is instead of calling it *business* networking, let's call it *prospect networking*, or Net Prospecting for short. Business networking implies we might be networking for many business reasons. Which again is great, but if we are networking solely for generating qualified leads, then I believe that Net Prospecting is more fitting. That stated, what are the benefits in leveraging the power of networks for prospecting purposes?

Build/ Expand the Contacts in Your Network

It is often said that being successful is 50% about who you know and 50% about who knows you. With networking you need both. Thus, networking helps you expand the raw numbers of contacts in your network. Additionally, Net Prospecting affords you the invaluable opportunity to make these new connections faster and easier as compared to other prospecting channels. This is particularly the case if you network at events such as business mixers or the type of after-work networking gatherings that many Chamber of Commerces and professional groups host regularly. Think of it this way. When you add a new person to your network, you actually increase your personal sphere of influence by a potential 250 people. That is if we use the 250-base number given by Joe Girard. Thus, the more people you add to your own network, the larger your potential reach increases exponentially.

Raises Profile Level

A second major benefit of networking is that it raises your individual and business profile. In other words, it gets you attention. Which from my perspective, is something that all businesses and sales professionals need if they are to conquer the problem of obscurity. **If not enough of your target market know you and what you do, then you run the risk of not selling enough of your product.** This happens even if you have the best product, the best service or the best price. Continuing along, raising one's profile means you become visible and get noticed. Whenever you attend networking events regularly, people will begin to recognize you. Next you begin to build your reputation as a knowledgeable, reliable, and supportive person. When this happen, you are now more likely to get more leads and referrals as you will be the source that comes to mind when others need or desire what you offer.

Discover Opportunities/ Generate More Sales

This is without a doubt the single most important reason why we prospect, and it is one of the greatest benefits in leveraging Net Prospecting. Think about it! Getting to know more people, building your contacts, having others know you, building relationships, connecting others together, all of these will naturally result in opportunities be it direct sales or viable referrals. And many times, these opportunities come when you least expect them. As a matter of fact, there are some businesses and sales professionals who believe that this benefit is so powerful they based their entire prospecting strategy on it.

But hold on, there are other benefits. I am referring to benefits such as being able to gain access to much needed advice that you might not have access to otherwise; increasing your level of confidence in yourself, your product offering, and how you relate with people; and increasing personal satisfaction from helping others.

But as great as Net Prospecting sounds, are there any cons?

Takes A Lot of Work

It should come as no surprise that the foundation of networking success is directly driven by either the *Golden Rule* or the *Platinum Rule*. For clarity, the *Golden Rule* states that we should treat others as we want to be treated while the *Platinum Rule* states that we should do unto others as *they* would want done to *them. Whichever rule you decide to use is entirely based on preference. The key point to remember, however, is that* all things being equal, people will do business with and refer business to, those people they know, like, and trust. Let me repeat, "... *know, like, and trust.*" At its core, successful Net Prospecting is about building, nurturing, and leveraging relationships. This knowing, liking, and trusting requires work, a lot of work.

But isn't this true of any relationship? Depending on the referenced source, relationships of all kinds can develop and prosper in stages ranging from as few as five to as many as eleven. The description of these stages is beyond the scope of this book. However, we do know that like any relationship, networking can also take time and be monotonous.

Takes A Lot of Time

Because Net Prospecting is ultimately about building relationships, and because it is this relationship-building that serves as the bridge that makes lead generation possible for Net Prospecting, it takes time to get it right, and to see consistent results. Sure, you might find some direct business or get a few great referrals immediately. But treat this as the exception not the rule. I have participated in a number of different referral networking groups for years. When I joined my first group, the leader impressed upon me the wisdom of looking at networking as a marathon rather than a sprint, because relationships take time. The *getting-to-know-folks* requires patience, and people are generally cautious – if not fearful – of networkers who only want to *get* first rather than *give* first. It will do you some good to heed the advice of the saying "we reap what we sow."

Can Become Monotonous

One of the criticisms that some sales professionals have of networking is that it can become monotonous with few rewards in the form of leads or business generated. Eventually you may see the same people over and over again. Therefore, it can seem like a waste of time. This criticism usually comes from the same sales professionals who have no problem calling the same prospects five, ten, fifteen times or more, often with important information, but other times calling or emailing just to "check in." The reality is that unless you have a transactional sales process and operate under a one-call close scenario, generating leads and winning business (even from those deemed high value) takes time. How long? Often about eight or more conversations to secure a deal. So to criticize networking as monotonous seems a little short sighted. Remember, Net Prospecting is about making connections and building relationships.

That stated, I do understand how seeing the same people over and over again can feel repetitious unless you have new bits of valuable information or new insights to share with the contacts each time. Also, having a different way of introducing yourself to others might be a way to break up the monotony.

Now that we have a pretty good idea of what Net Prospecting is, as well as some of its major benefits and disadvantages, let's move to the next point, which is the goal of networking.

Goal of Networking

What are the goals or objectives for engaging in Net Prospecting? The answer is fairly simple. Like all other channels, the goal is and always should be to generate qualified leads, a.k.a. sales ready opportunities or prospects). However, depending upon if you take a hunting approach or farming approach, how you go about achieving this goal can be very different. Full disclosure; although I do see how a sales professional might use the hunting approach to find opportunities that he could close and win today, he will experience so much push-back that he will ultimately turn off too many potential prospects by using this approach. Trust me! I had to learn this lesson the hard way. Like many great networkers, eventually I had to understand and appreciate the underlying rules that networking is about making connections, building relationships, giving value first, and selling second. So, for Net Prospecting, **the best approach to take is the farming approach**. This is when you do a lot of nurturing and developing to get the opportunity ripe enough for harvesting.

Net Prospecting Strategy

Now that we have addressed the best approach in general, let's discuss some key tips that make the best use of Net Prospecting. The following are seven great tips that are very well-tested by me, as well as many of the clients I have trained.

1. **Attend the right events**. Let's face it. To get good at networking you must start networking. You can begin anytime, anywhere. It is not time- or location-specific. Business networking can take place in the doctor's office; while waiting in line for coffee; at your kid's basketball game. These are unstructured, unplanned networking opportunities, and they happen more often than you realize. There are also the more structured, planned networking events that you might find your Local Chamber of Commerce, or other business organizations. To find them, search online at sites like: *www.meetup.com*; *www.eventbrite.com*; *www.linkedIn.com* (Groups in LinkedIn host networking events); *www.networkafterwork.com*; just to name a few. I recommend you **plan to attend two to three networking events each week**. Put them on your calendar, and then actually attend at least one to two per week.

2. **Know how to introduce yourself to strangers**. The majority of networking events attendees have the same goal as you with respect to making new contacts and growing existing contacts. Consequently, it is relatively easy for you to get into conversations, because you already have something in common. Even so, make sure you introduce yourself to everyone you meet. We covered how to draft and deliver the Elevator Pitch or the Thirty-Second Introduction. Use this introduction regardless of the situation (meeting in person, speaking on the phone, sending an email, mailing a letter, or any other form of initial communication).

3. **Know how to engage a person in a conversation**. The only way to engage someone in a conversation is to ask questions. He who asks questions dictates the pace and direction of the conversation. The first rule of networking is to listen twice as much as you speak. When you do speak, ask open-ended questions, such as "How did you get started in your business?" or "What do you enjoy most about your profession?" or "What are the key points that separate your company from your competition?" or "How has the recent legislature on XYZ affected your business?" These are just a few examples. Typically, ask no more than three to four questions. But most importantly, be conversational. Don't act as though you are interrogating the person. Remember, the goal is to make a connection, do some preliminary pre-qualification, and get the person to form great thoughts that lead to a favorable emotional impression of you.

4. **Know how to segway out of a conversation so you can move to the next contact**. At some point, you need to gracefully exit the conversation and move on to a new contact. Make sure you do this with the same degree of professionalism and friendliness that you did to open the conversation. Before existing, make sure that you have the new contact's business card. If asked, give your card as well. Finally, tell the person to expect a follow up from you based on the agreed upon next step.

5. **Enter all contact information and conversation notes in your CRM.** Either the same day, or the very next morning, make sure you enter all your new contact information into your CRM. Make sure

you add any pertinent information and intel you learned during the initial conversation. Also schedule any pending follow-ups. Do all of this before you move on to anything else. Do not, I repeat, *do not* file the cards away with the goal of entering this information into the CRM later. Do not leave them just sitting on your desk. Trust me. If you don't do this data entry and follow-up immediately, you will get too busy and forget to do it later. Thus, ensuring that the time you spent at the event, as well as all the great new contacts you made, become lost opportunities.

6. **Connect with the new contact via social media**. Search for the person on LinkedIn, Facebook, Twitter, and any other social site that is applicable to your target market. You will be surprised at the number of new contacts that easily accept your request to connect via social media based solely upon you having met them at a networking event. Also, this connection gives you the ability to learn a little more about the new contact and see what degree of commonality the two of you already have.

7. **Finally, get your follow-up done on time**. For example, if your follow-up is to set a one-on-one meeting or call, do it ASAP. You want to always strike while the iron is hot, or while the initial conversation is still fresh in the mind of the contact.

The above seven steps are just a few things you can do immediately to get the biggest bang out of your networking efforts. By no means are these tips the only ones you want to master. If you want more tips, or if you decide to learn a lot more on Net Prospecting, feel free to reach out directly to us by phone or email. We will be honored to discuss your needs and provide the "right fit" solution. You can find contact information on our website.

13: Social Prospecting

Social Media is the ultimate equalizer.
It gives a voice and a platform to anyone willing to engage.

– AMY JO MARTIN –

Social Selling is an umbrella term that includes activities like social listening, social monitoring, Social Prospecting, sharing relevant content, and personal branding. Social Prospecting is when you use social media to prospect and generate qualified leads or sales-ready opportunities. While Social Prospecting is the relatively *new guy in town*, it is quickly becoming one of the most effective means of generating highly qualified, sales-ready opportunities. Consider these stats:

1. Forty-five percent of salespeople now use social media in their prospecting efforts, and more so in the pre-call research phase.[1]

2. Thirty-nine percent of B2B sales professionals who use social media in prospecting (and selling) reduced the amount of time they spent researching accounts and contacts.[1]

3. Thirty-three percent of B2B sales reps report that social selling increases the number of leads they have to work with.[2]

4. Seventy-six percent of buyers are ready to have a social media conversation with potential providers.[3]

5. **Sales professionals who use social media tools in prospecting (and selling) see 45% more sales opportunities.**[3]

6. Thirty-one percent of B2B professionals report that social selling tools allow them to build deeper relationships with clients.

7. IDC found that 75% of B2B buyers and 84% of executives use contacts and information from social networks as part of their purchase process.[4]

8. Sixty-four percent of teams that used social media hit their quota compared to 49% of teams that did not use social media tools hit their quota.[4]

It is hard to argue the impact and power of Social Prospecting. Which is why it is important to leverage Social Prospecting as part of the communication stack when attempting to generate qualified leads. There are many in the Social Selling 2.0 world that extol the virtues of Social Prospecting (and social selling in general) as a sign that cold-calling is dead. These social selling enlightened ones argue that there is no longer the need to make an unexpected, interruptive, and intrusive phone call even again. But these gurus fail to consider that any outreach be it social, email, face-to-face, SMS, phone call, or any unexpected outreach is still a cold call, regardless of it being from a known or unknown source.

If you were to Google the phrase "social selling and the death of the traditional sale," you will find a blog post written by Katie King. At least at the time of writing this book, it was the top search result. In her post, Katie writes, "in this digital age, the traditional salesman is dying. Cold sales, hard sales are a thing of the past. Nobody wants to listen to a scripted phone pitch or give up time to listen to a sales pitch."[5] Like many bold claims, there are some truths to this statement, but there is also more when you consider it fully.

Like all possible channels for prospecting, be it Tele Prospecting, Email Prospecting, SMS Prospecting, and yes, Social Prospecting, a sales professional can take either a hunting or farming approach. Using social media for prospecting is no different.

One of the major schools of thought regarding social selling is the idea that a sale professional SHOULD first seek to build a relationship with potential prospects, engaging them in social conversation, and adding value, before ever seeking to sell. This is the farming approach to social selling. The goal is to build that all important familiarity with you, your business, your brand, your product. This MUST be developed first, then and only then, should selling take place; this is when you make an outreach to begin a sales conversation. According to social selling advocates, this is the reason why social selling replaces traditional selling as the primary means of generating leads, making sales, and servicing customers. No one likes to be pitched, no one wants to be interrupted to take a unplanned call from a salesperson, and no one likes the hard sell. There are a number of companies who use social selling as its only (or at least primary) means of generating prospects and acquiring new customers. In her book *The Art of Social Selling* Shannon Belew has a case study on the Internet-based company Shopify. According to Mark Hayes, head of public relations for Shopify, the company uses social media as the primary means of acquiring new customers.[6]

Granted, Social Prospecting is less intrusive, and like emailing, less threatening. After all no one is going to hang up on you, or curse at you, tell you never to call back, shut the door in your face, or scream and tell you to get out of his/her office. Yet when all is said and done, unless you are going to wait for the prospect to contact you, you will still have to make some unexpected and unplanned outreach to that prospect – with or without familiarity. That outreach can take the form of a telephone call, email, text, and yes, social options like inmails, direct messages, and tweets. Social selling does not completely eliminate the need to make an "unexpected" outreach to have a sales conversation, unless your aim is to get the buyer to initiate the sales conversation (generating inbound leads).

While you might be able to survive as a small company with relying on just inbound leads, for larger companies and for companies looking to aggressively grown in clients and/or revenue, the quantity of leads generated from this inbound marketing rarely is enough. Therefore, an unexpected outreach strategy is necessary. And from this, using Social Prospecting DOES warm the outreach (meaning that at least, the prospect is familiar with you). Remember, the two greatest challenges with cold-calling is making an unexpected outreach and doing so with little or no familiarity. Social Prospecting attempts to resolve the no-familiarity challenge.

To be clear, the goal of this section is not to establish Social Prospecting as the "magic elixir" that cures all that is wrong with prospecting. But rather, to inject some pragmatism into the discussion by listing major benefits AND challenges, as well as outlining some steps that leverage the potential of Social Prospecting so that you generate enough high quality prospects.

Top Benefits in Using Social Prospecting

One of the major benefits in leveraging social media for prospecting is that it gives you access to hundreds to thousands of possible buyers that you would not have access otherwise due to time, distance, and other limiting factors. Such access is obtained without paying thousands of dollars to purchase a targeted list from a data broker. It cost nothing to have a Facebook account, to create a Facebook Fan Page, to have a Twitter account or a LinkedIn account. Yes, you do have to pay a few dollars for LinkedIn Premium, but this cost can be as a low as $49 a month.

Additionally, you can purchase a tool like Hootsuite to build your targeted list and leverage the full power of that list. Like LinkedIn, the cost is margin. With Hootsuite, you can purchase the basis plan for as low as $19 per month for a single account to $500 a month for an account with up to fifty account profiles. That's still considerably less than purchasing a data file.

As a final note on this benefit, one of the challenges of buying a targeted list from a data broker is the integrity of the data. It is all too common to get bad or outdated contact formation and duplicates. This is not as much a factor with Social Prospecting, at least not in my experience. The contact information and other related company data on the desired targets tends to be more up-to-date when you curate it yourself from social media.

A second major benefit with Social Prospecting is that that it allows you to build familiarly by using the wealth of personal and private information that prospects reveal about themselves on social media. In 2012, Cheryl Connor wrote an article for Forbes[7] in which she pointed out how (to the disadvantage of our privacy) people willfully and accidentally share too much information or the wrong information on social media. Ms. Connor lists case after case, in which the disclosure of such private information costs some individuals their jobs, causes loss in competitive advantage (by revealing trades secrets), leads to embarrassment, and in one case resulted in criminal charges. Reputation Defender, wrote a similar blog post that gave examples of how so much embarrassing information was shared.[8] Be that as it may, as a sales professional you can legally use a lot of that intel to build a much better understanding of your potential buyers, get connected faster, and build that all important relationship. You can do all of this faster than ever without ever meeting the person or leaving the comforts of your office.

A third major benefit is the ease of which you can set up a sales conversation or appointment to encourage potential prospects to perform a desired call to action (CTA). According to our research, you are 4.2 times more likely to get an appointment if there is a personal connection with a buyer.

Challenges in Using Social Prospecting

The list of possible benefits to leveraging Social Prospecting are many. However, there are also many challenges, as well. These challenges can be as simple as developing a Social Prospecting strategy, knowing how Social Prospecting fits into your prospecting mix, and knowing which social media platforms to leverage. But key among these challenges are how to:

1. Determine the amount of time to invest

2. Decide which platform to use

3. Measure your effectiveness

Let's face it, Social Prospecting is time consuming, at least to get good enough to generate highly qualified leads. This is because Social Prospecting, like Net Prospecting, is social in nature. And it does not matter if you are hunting or farming. As a farmer using Social Prospecting your initial goals is to increase familiarity, build a relationship, present yourself a credible and valuable resource. You do these before you attempt to sell. This by its very nature is time-consuming. In her book *The Art of Social Selling* Shannon Belew quotes a report from Forrester Researching stating, "B2B Marketer must nurture prospects for months or years before they turn into sales opportunities..."[9] The reality is that to really be effective at Social Prospecting, you must be willing to invest time each week to do the work, and be patient, because the results improve over time. In short, while the ROI for Social Prospecting is high, it is not immediate and can take up to six months to see a return.

There are literally hundreds of potential social media platforms that you can use to generate leads. But deciding on which social media platform to use can be daunting. Unless you have been living under a rock for the past decade, I am sure you are aware of Facebook, LinkedIn, Twitter as three of the top platforms. But did you know that there are hundreds of similar platforms on the market today? An article published on Small Business Trends[10] list twenty of the most popular social media sites. These of course include Facebook, LinkedIn, and Twitter, but also Google+, YouTube, Pinterest, Instagram, Tumblr, and Flickr just to name a few. Another site, Practical Ecommerce, lists "105 leading Social Networks Worldwide."[11] With such a large number of possible sites, I know what you may be asking: "Should I be on all of them? If not, then which ones should I be on?" The answer is simple. Be on the same sites as your targets. For example, while Facebook has reportedly close to two billion users, and Instagram closely follows, 65% of B2B sales professional use LinkedIn as their primarily social media platform.[12]

If you engage in B2C sales, then it makes a lot of sense for you to be on Facebook and Instagram. That stated, if you find that your prospects are on one platform or five platforms, you should want to pick from those, as well. However, for the sake of time, narrow that possible list down to two or three. This would allow you to spend enough time and maximize your ROI without spreading yourself too thin.

Lastly, how do you know if your Social Prospecting efforts are generating a return? The simple answer is another question: *Do your activities lead to an increase in qualified opportunities for your sales process?* When prospecting, we constantly looking for prospects that are better qualified, much further along in the buying process, near to closing, and have better margins. Because of the time factor, and the sheer number of possible platforms available to you, the challenge is ensuring that you spend your time wisely and use the right tool. To help resolve this issue, a number of companies have developed tools for measuring your social selling effectiveness.

LinkedIn, however, has developed what it calls the "first-of-its kind social selling measurement"[13] called the Social Selling Index (SSI). According to LinkedIn, this Social Selling Index scores on a scale of zero to one hundred based on your LinkedIn activities relating to the four pillars of social selling. In their internal study they found a strong correlation between achieving sales goals and sales reps with a high SSI. These finding state the following:

- Reps with a strong SSI had 45% more sales opportunities
- Reps with a strong SSI were 51% more likely to hit quota
- Reps with a strong SSI had outsold peers who don't use social media by 78%
- Reps with a strong SSI were three times more likely to go to [president's] club

Interesting? LinkedIn gives you the ability to find out for FREE what your SSI is. So, I ran the report and found that my SSI was 79.

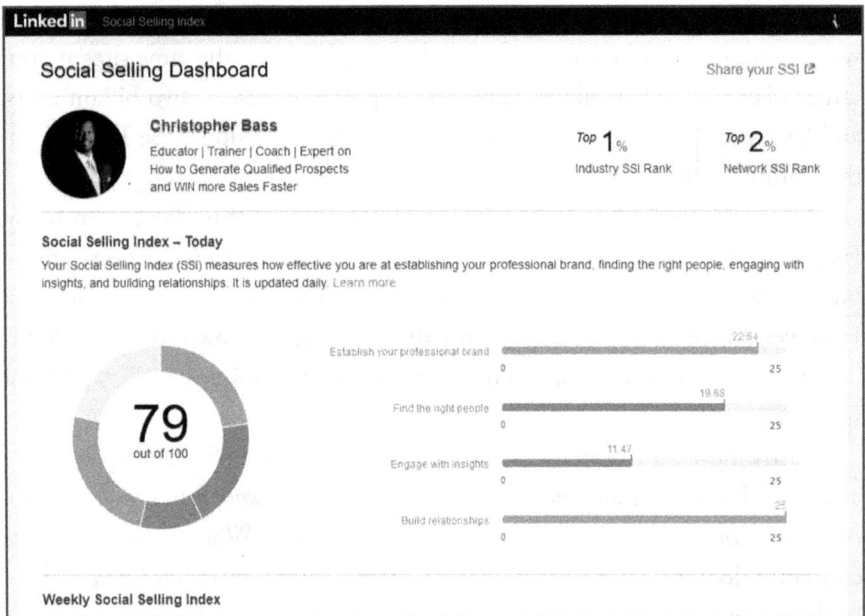

Klout

Founded in 2008 by Joe Fernandez and Binh Tran, Klout is a website and mobile app that uses social media analytics to rate its users according to online social influence via the "Klout Score."[14] Klout uses various sources like Bing, Facebook, Foursquare, Google+, Instagram, LinkedIn, Twitter, YouTube, and Wikipedia data to create Klout user profiles that assign a unique Klout score. Klout scores range from one to one hundred, with higher scores corresponding to a higher ranking of the breadth and strength of one's online social influence. According to the website Brandwatch.com, author Ruxandra Mindruta reviewed Klout and nine other social media monitoring tools, and she asserts that Klout is probably one of the most controversial. There are those who hate it and claim that its scoring system is completely inaccurate. And trying to interact with this group is an impossible mission."[15]

Then there are others. For example, TweetReach monitors how far your tweets travel, measuring the actual impact and implications of social media discussions. Buzzsumo is an excellent way to analyze and monitor your Facebook pages. Along with metrics for each post, Buzzsumo gives you the ability to see what content performs best. Likealyzer is a free tool that allows you to analyze your Facebook page, giving you a good roundup of stats with some benchmarking.

Tips on How to Use Social Prospecting

Hopefully by now you know that with prospecting in general there are four major steps that you must execute if you want to generate prospects; these include finding, contacting, engaging, and qualifying prospects. The same four steps apply to Social Prospecting. To execute each of these steps effectively requires a number of sub-steps if you are to harness the power of Social Prospecting and have a funnel full of opportunities that you can close in the shortest time possible.

1. **Know what you want to accomplish with social media**. Are you looking to use social media as just a research tool to gather intel on possible prospects? Are you looking to use it as a means of building relationships? Will you use it to establish direct contact? Or are you looking turn introductions from existing contacts into "pipeline contacts"? Remember the old saying. To achieve what you want, you must first be clear on what you want.

2. **Know which platform to use for generating prospects and measuring your effectiveness.** Remember, if you operate in the B2B space, then LinkedIn and Twitter are better sites for you. Contrastingly, if you operate in the B2C space, you may find Facebook, Instagram, and Pinterest to be a much better match. The point is to make sure you understand your targets and know which

social media platforms your targets will most likely be on. If you find you need help in making this determination, you can go back to the previous sections of this chapter that lists various resources. Or, if you prefer a guided approach, contact my office.

3. **Inventory existing content and develop additional content**. In Social Prospecting content is key. Shannon Belew argues that "sharing high quality content through your social channel is the foundation for building a relationship with your potential customers."[16] While this content can take many forms (from testimonials, Q&As, Infographics, Polls and Surveys and videos) it must be relevant to the prospect. Developing contact is pretty straight-forward. You can do a web search for tips. If you are desiring more of a hands-on approach, then give us a call and we can discuss your needs.

4. **Develop an outreach schedule**. Generate a schedule of social media posts you will use to start the social conversation. This should include posting fresh content, commenting on existing content, starting conversation with new contacts and/or engaging new influencers. Examples of one schedule outlined by Shannon Belew is a 3/2/3/1. This include sharing three new posts, engaging with two new influencers, sharing three links and commenting on at least one group thread, article, or blog. The key here is to get involved in social conversations and provide value in every conversation you interact.

5. **Budget time wisely**. Because developing success with Social Prospecting takes time to see an ROI, and requires a lot of work, it is best to set aside time each day to do Social Prospecting in smaller segments rather than trying to do it all at once. Devoting just one hour of time to Social Prospecting is recommended by social selling experts. This one hour of time gives you the ability to do social monitoring, engage in social conversation, and post new content to your relevant social media sites. My strong recommendation is to schedule this time outside your prime prospecting time.

6. **Log or document all Social Prospecting activities in our CRM to find out what impact Social Prospecting has on lead generation**. Remember like every other prospecting channel that we have discussed throughout this book, the goal with Social Prospecting

is to generate prospects. Like Net Prospecting, Social Prospecting demands that you take a farming approach. This means doing a lot of connecting and relationship-building. As such, it is very easy to get sidetracked with the relationship-building at the expense of generating qualified leads. As direct as this may sound, as prospectors, we do not build relationships for relationship sake. Instead we build relationships that eventually yield sales opportunities for our prospect pipeline. Therefore, logging and documenting all Social Prospecting activities provide you with objective data to analyze to determine which activities lead to opportunities and which ones might be time wasters.

The above steps do not comprise an exhaustive list one should take to begin leveraging the power of Social Prospecting to generate your "bottomless funnel" of highly qualified leads. Instead, we need to look at this list as just a start. I highly recommend you invest more time in learning more, acquiring new skills, and applying new methods that will give you the best ROI with Social Prospecting.

14: Which Channel
is Better?

*One of the most important things that I have learned in my 57 years
is that life is all about choices. On every journey you take, you face
choices. At every fork in the road, you make a choice.
And it is those decisions that shape our lives.*

– MIKE DEWINE –

We have all heard the old adage, "Never put all your eggs in one basket."
Meaning, it is best to diversify your options and put some eggs in different baskets. This is where the Concept of Diversification in investment comes into play as a way of managing risks. According to the website Investopedia, "the rationale behind this technique contends that a portfolio constructed of different kinds of investments will, on average, yield higher returns and pose a lower risk than any individual investment found within the portfolio."[1] Logically, of course, this makes sense.

On the other hand, we have also heard the saying, "jack of all trades, yet master of none." Meaning, you have a person who is good or adept at a lot of things but is not necessary a specialist at any one thing. Depending upon your particular way of thinking, you may be someone who believes that being a generalist generates a lower ROI compared to being a specialist. Yet, isn't the concept of diversification based on the same "jack of all trades" concept?

It is commonly accepted that high levels of success come from being a specialist rather than a generalist. As a matter of fact, many of the people we admire today for their high levels of success are those who were specialists, not generalists. Think of Michael Jordan, Bill Gates, Steffi Graf, Albert Einstein, Mother Teresa, Mahatma Gandhi, Vince Lombardi, or even Jesus Christ, himself. These greats were all specialists in their own fields. Many excellent motivational and inspirational leaders such as Tony Robbins, Eric Thomas, and Jim Rohn have all advocated the same.

Confusing right? So, the question becomes who is right? Which strategy should you take when deciding which prospecting channels, you will leverage in your quest to generate a pipeline of highly qualified leads? After all, you can't do both, right? Well, **the answer to this question depends upon your level of risk tolerance**. The higher your risk tolerance, the more likely you are to take the "all eggs in one basket approach." The less risk tolerant you are, the greater likelihood you will take a more diversified approach. It is true that if you focus on one thing solely and completely, you have a greater chance of being successful faster than if you focus on multiple things at the same time. But it is also true that you run the risk of failing miserably if that one option does not work out. If the failure is great enough, such a failure could set you back much further than where you originally started. It is also equally true that taking a diversification approach does not guarantee success. Moreover, opting for a diversified approach has the potential of taking slightly longer to reach the coveted destination compared to the single approach. The point? The answer is not a simple one.

Have I made everything more confusing? Ultimately, the decision on what channel strategy to select should be based on a few other factors besides level of risk tolerance. For starters, I recommend that you conduct some research and speak with others in your profession who have "been there, done that." Doing so provides you with feedback regarding what may have worked and not worked for them and why. Next, I recommend that you ask lots of questions and study the research. Finally, you must make the decision based on what you believe is most likely to work. Whatever you decide, you must be willing to stick to the plan for at least ninety days before changing or modifying your direction.

The Four Critical Steps

PART III

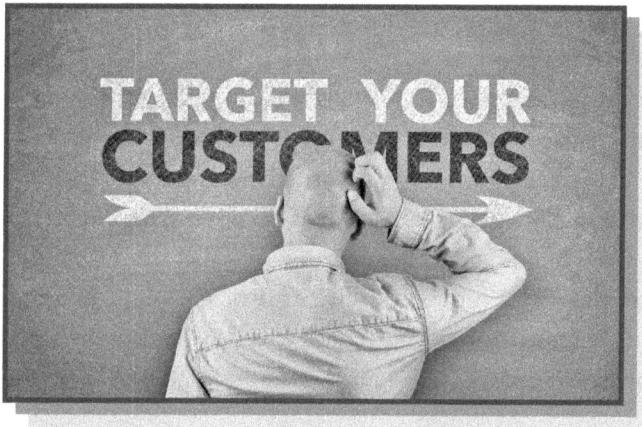

15: The Find

If you aim at nothing, you will hit it every time.

– ZIG ZIGLAR –

One of the most important prospecting questions to ask yourself centers around *who*. Who are you (or should be) targeting? In other words, which buyer is mostly likely to need, want, desire your products? Who is most likely to buy now or later? Who are you trying to get in front of? Who are you trying to contact? You can also look at this from the perspective of who do you want to do business with? The answers to these questions ultimately depends upon finding potential buyers who have the problems, needs, desires, goals, interests, and/or pains that you're offering can help with. While the answers to these questions are pretty straightforward, far too many sales professionals, and businesses, start prospecting AND promoting without a clear picture of whom they must target.

Target Market Defined

Finding your prospects requires that you have a clear indication of who your target market is. According to the American Marketing Association, "a target market is a particular portion of the total population which is identified as the ones most likely to purchase your products or services."[1] This target market is most likely to purchase because it falls into a broad category of people who can use, but not necessarily want to buy, your products or services. For example, if you are selling heavy duty construction equipment, then school teachers, housewives, children, and college kids would not be your target, However, someone in the building and demolishing of structures would be. Or if you sell software that helps businesses solve a particular problem around logistics and tracking shipment, then your target would be logistics companies or any freight-moving business.

Shotgun vs. Rifle

Generally speaking, there are two broad approaches you could consider when identifying your targets; the shotgun approach and the rifle approach. The shotgun approach or "the casting a wide net" is a broad strategy that seeks to sell any and everything that is within reach. In hunting for game, a shotgun approach isn't necessarily used to hit a specific target, but to hit all targets that are near or in close proximity of each other. A shotgun approach in targeting prospects is done in the same vein. Here you attempt to target and appeal to a wide market of potential customers. This situation occurs when the target audience is too diverse to focus on any one segment.

Taking a shotgun approach can be a very effective strategy for companies with a large budgets or for companies in which the target demographics is huge, as was the case for American Alliance of Ethical Movers[2] However, for smaller companies with a limited budget and a limited number of solutions, taking a shotgun approach can bankrupt the business or cause collateral damage. Granted, taking a shotgun approach will net you some hits and even some kills, but how much ammunition, how much money, and how much effort will you expend in the process? More importantly, taking the shotgun approach might result in winning customers that later turn out to be profit piranhas at the worst or just outright bad customers at best.

In contrast, the rifle approach is more focused, and narrower in scope and scale. Instead of trying to target indiscriminately all birds, a rifle approach seeks to focus on specific, high-yield prospects. The rifle approach seeks to narrow down this target market so as to have a laser focus. The rifle approach tends to use highly personal communication messages, direct one-to-one calls, emails texts, faxes, and letters.

Rabbits, Deer, and Elephants

When I first got started in sales some twenty years ago, I use to hear fellow sales reps speak and debate about the value of hunting elephants, buffalo, deer, and rabbits. At the time, I had always felt these conversations and debates were meaningless. I mean, as salespeople we are not hunting animals, right? We are out to win new business anyway we can. Later, when I got into software sales, again I ran into this debate. However, this time it was in the context of determining the size of the deal (in terms of revenue) and the amount of time, effort, and resources necessary to win these various deal sizes.

Intrigued, I did some research on these terms so that I could have the best understanding and execution of them within my own selling efforts. This is what I discovered many years ago. In general, Elephants, also known as Whales in some industries, refer to those large, enterprise deals that come around rarely. When they do, however, and you and your team win them, such a win can help out tremendously. Investopdia.com explains it this way: "If a company is able to close an 'elephant' sale, then it may see a significant positive impact on its revenues, especially if it is able to obtain a multi-year contract."[3] Contrastingly, Rabbits are micro deals. While being significantly smaller, they are more plentiful than Elephants. Additionally, Rabbits do not take as long to hunt and kill because they tend to be everywhere. Great, right?

Well, not so fast. Despite this ubiquitous nature of Rabbits, you need to hunt and capture a sizable amount of them to reap the same benefit as you would in capturing that Elephant. If you need to just feed yourself, then you don't need that many Rabbits. But if you have to feed an entire village, an entire company, then you need hundreds or thousands of Rabbits. This very fact means you may end up taking the same amount of time and consume the same amount of resources in both captures.

Finally, Deer are medium size game. They are not as abundant as Rabbits yet are seen more often than Elephants. While Deer take slightly longer to hunt and capture than Rabbits, hunting time for a single Deer is much less than it takes to hunt for an Elephant. Again, if you need to capture only a single Deer, then that time is negligible. But if you need to capture a lot of Deer, equal to the impact of an Elephant, then you may find that this hunting of a lot of Deer requires more time, energy, and resources.

That stated, are you ready to hunt? In all seriousness, you may ask which prospect deal size is a better target? After all, the subject of Elephants, Deer, and Rabbits is an essential **discussion about the size of the customers you desire to target**. Believe it or not, but the simple answer to the above questions depends on whether you must eat now, or if you can wait and eat later. If you need to eat now, then you better start hunting Rabbits. Otherwise, you will starve to death. If you don't NEED to eat now, then the next question to answers is this: *Do you have the skills, the resources, and the time to take down big game?* If so, then maybe you should target the Elephants. Remember though, if you hunt Elephants, you will need to take the rifle approach. Whereas when hunting Deer and especially Rabbits, a shotgun approach is more fitting. Lastly keep in mind to hunt Elephants, or any big deal, generally requires a considerate amount of resources. Thus, hunting and capturing big game tends to be a team endeavor.

Look-alike Companies

Instead of just looking at the relative size of a potential target, you could also consider look-alike companies. If you run a business that is operational now, you can make this targeting easier by simply pursuing companies/individuals that look like your best customers. These look-alike targets are your best customers either because they generate the highest return, or because they are less of a strain on your support resources, or because their needs (and what your product offers) are a perfect fit. Because of this value, it is highly advisable that you leverage this intel and target potential customers who look like your current customers; because selling them on the value of your offer, and on why they should do business with you, is easier due to reference-based selling. This last aspect is generally referred to as closing or working "the low hanging fruit."

Market Research

The look-a-like company approach to targeting new prospects is applicable only if you have existing customers. If you, however, are just starting out, you will need to conduct some research on who the best target is based on some known and unknown factors. You can ask yourself the question of who is my solution ideally designed for? Who was the target that I had in mind as the "ideal" buyer for this product? One common way of getting these questions answered is (and has been) to hire a market research company to conduct your research in the form of surveys or focus groups. This option, however, can be very pricey. So be extremely careful in going this route. Alternatively, you could use an inhouse group to conduct this research. That is, if you have an existing team in place. If no existing team, then you can very well conduct this research yourself.

Gut Decision

Rabbits, Deer, Whales, Elephants? Look-alike Companies, Marketing Research? All this may sound too complicated. Is there anything less complex? Yes! One alternative is follow your instincts; take the Gut-Decision approach. Unless you have no prior experience with the products or buyers for your product, common sense dictates that you should have some notion of who your ideal prospect is, might be, or should be. In other words, you should have some very clear ideas and knowledge of who you want to do business with. From there, you can use that as the basis of targeting. Just remember that you might have to make some adjustments to this as you begin to execute and get some information/intel that might prove valuable.

Narrowing Your Focus

Whichever approach you use, make sure that you narrow your focus as best you can. Defining a target market just based on a broad category is not focused and not specific enough. To target effectively, your target market must also fit some predefined criteria, also known as qualification factors. Let's say you have a product that helps organizations deal with the complex proposal process involved in doing business with the federal government. Let's also say that your product is offered only in English and does not take into account any international laws or compliance factors. In this case, you look for just those companies that deal with U.S.-based governmental proposals and contracts that do business in English.

The point of this conversation is to overemphasize the importance of narrowly defining your target. Remember, the more defined your target market is, the more likely you are to hit it. That is because the more focus you bring to the task, the better the results you achieve. Conversely, the larger the targeted audience, the greater the resources you need to have to reach this target. Keep this in mind. All potential prospects are not created equally. Target the best leads so you get the best ROI on your prospecting efforts.

Specific Demographic Factors

It is said that if you don't know what you are looking for, how will you ever find it? Or if you don't know where you are going, any road will get you there. What these sayings imply is that if you are to hit your target, you must first know what/who you are aiming for. Easier said than done, right?

In a way, *no*. You, can however, start by answering the following questions.

1. **Are you targeting people versus businesses, government agencies, or non-profits?** If you are targeting businesses, are there certain types of business based on structure? Think of sole proprietors, partnerships, corporations, etc.

2. **Are you targeting based on size (small, medium, large)?** Industry classification? Number of employees? Annual revenue? Geographical locations? Local, national international, or within a certain mile radius of a zip code?

3. **Are you targeting specific individuals?** Is there a certain targeted income, education, marital status, occupation, racial group, or age that you're going after? The more narrowly you define your target market the better chances you have to find them.

Defining Too Narrowly

Not narrowly defining your target market can be a waste of time, money, and effort. But defining too narrowly can be costly, as well. If you define too narrowly, you run the risk of having a universe of prospects so small that the only way for you to survive as a business would be capture 100% of the market share. While this might be a great goal to aspire to, 100% market share is highly improbable.

Knowing the Right Party Contact

Knowing whom to target as potential buyers is the first step. However, knowing who (the right party) you should you be contacting is equally important.

In other words, do you need to speak with anyone in particular? Are there very specific people, with a particular title or role, with whom you should speak regarding the challenges or problems that your solution addresses? Is there a particular person in the organization who is impacted the most? My selling career has been mostly, if not entirely, devoted to selling to business (B2B). Thus, I don't know how important it is for me to know who the right party contact (RPC) is or the appropriate contact (AC) for consumers. But for B2B prospecting this point is huge. In knowing who to target, you need to know who makes the decision on what and whether to buy.

Are you offering a product that helps Purchasing Departments? If so, then shouldn't you be targeting the Head of Purchasing? Are you offering a product that helps sales teams improve production or drive sales results? If so, then your RPC is most likely the VP of Sales or Head of Sales. Does your product help businesses define and set a clear Strategic Vision? If so, then your RPC might be the CEO, President, Owner or Executive Director. The point here is to emphasize the need to know who the best contact is in your targeted company.

Compiling a List of Names

Once you have narrowly defined your target, and once you know who the RPC is, it is advisable that you compile a list of names. Instead of finding a single contact and then attempting to contact and engage that one person, compiling a list of all contacts enables you to prospect more effectively and efficiently.

In creating this list, you want to ensure that you have all the pertinent information as follows:

1. Contact information
2. Direct dial numbers
3. Mobile numbers
4. Fax numbers
5. Email addresses
6. Links to social media profiles

The above points are just a start. You might find that you also need to know the type of business structure, the annual revenues, the number of locations, and the number of employees. Any additional information you need in order to generate leads for your sales funnel, is information you need to get.

There are few ways you can compile this list.

1. Compile it yourself
2. Purchase it directly from list or data brokers (i.e., companies like Hoovers or Info USA)
3. Obtain it from your local Chamber of Commerce or any organization that has a compiled list for sale

If you generate or compile this list yourself, be mindful that this process requires some time, takes legwork and digging. This time is considerably more compared to buying a list; however, the accuracy of the data contain in your self-compiled list is far superior to those of a purchased list.

Obtaining Email Addresses

Outside of texting, emailing is the second most commonly-used means of communication. It is what a lot of salespeople use, and it is one of the preferred methods of initial communication by many B2B buyers. In a super-connected, highly busy world, a large number of people prefer emailing to taking or making phone calls. Thus, having a person's email address is like gold. There are a number of web-based companies like RocketReach.co, Silk Prospector, Hunter, and Clearbit Connect where you can gather email addresses with varying degrees of accuracy. Some work as Chrome extensions, like Silk Prospector, some work as a free Gmail plugin, while others like RocketReach permit you to search a name, company or LinkedIn profile URL to retrieve emails. RocketReach also gives you links to your searched contact's social media profiles.

Leveraging Various Communication Channels

I don't see the sensibility in using SMS messaging, faxing, or direct mail as an efficient means of finding the RPC and obtaining contact information. Tele Prospecting into the organization, conducting In-Person visits, leveraging In-Person and Social Networking, and Email Prospecting are all viable tools that when leveraged correctly help you build your list of potential buyers.

Calling into the Organization

Sometimes despite your Herculean efforts to find the RPC's contact information, you might still be left with nothing verifiable. In this situation, I have found that calling into the organization is highly effective. With this method you simply call into the organization and ask the receptionist (or the person's admin assistant) for this information. Granted, you might not get it all the time, but you may be surprised to find that with the right tone, at the right time, to the right person, you are able to get this important data. I normally use this as second or third option when my primary option has failed to deliver.

Structure a Script for the Call

To make this call successfully, there are generally four things that you must include in a call script to ensure you get the desired information.

1. Start with the introduction
2. Ask for help
3. State the requested information you seek
4. Thank the person and hang up

See the sample script below for an example.

Script 1

Hi! My name is Christopher. I am calling from Company XYZ. How are you?

Do you mind if I asked a question?

Does your company have any of the following? Inside sales team? Business Development team?

Yes? Great! What is the name of the person who makes decisions regarding the training and development of these teams?

Hey, Thanks! (Make sure to get the full spelling of the names. Once confirmed see if you can also get a direct connect number or an extension.)

In-Person Visits

You can also use In-Person Prospecting to find out who the RPC is and obtain vital intel about the organization at the same time. More often, this typically involves speaking with the gatekeeper, receptionist, or security guard. If you manage to get into the office, past security, past the past a gatekeeper, you might be able to speak directly with other workers to gather as much information as you can. This last technique is commonly referred to as "walking in the back door." Similar to using the phone to call into the organization, this is a very powerful alternative, because in additional to getting the information, there are times when you bump into the intended contact. Consequently, you might need to be prepared to seize the opportunity and have an impromptu meeting with the person.

Emailing Another Person

Emailing a person for whom you DO have contact information in order to obtain the contact information of your desired account is another strategy. Many SaaS (Software-as-a-Service) based companies with Business Development Rep (BDR) teams or Sales Development Reps (SDR) teams leverage this method considerably. Here your goal is to get an internal referral. Once you obtain this information, you can follow up and initiate contact with the RPC.

Using Net Prospecting

Once of the great benefits of In-Person Networking (as opposed to Social Networking) is that you can quickly build a contact list of potential buyers. This is true when done in structured networking events. In reality, 99.99% of the folks in attendance are also there to meet new people. So unless you are completely offensive or repulsive in appearance, obtaining business cards of the attendees is easy. Thus, getting the right contacts for you list is also very easy.

Be mindful, however, that not everyone you meet at these events is a potential prospect. But many of those who are not possible buyers right now may turn out to be valuable resources that can connect you with others in their organizations or networks.

Using Social Media to Build a List

You can use a number of different social media platforms to build prospecting lists of potential targeted companies and individuals. This can be done directly and indirectly. Twitter gives you the ability to build targeted lists. LinkedIn has the Sales Navigator program, which lets you build list of target contacts, It also let you see your potential prospects' contact information if available. With the indirect approach you leverage the existing contacts you have on these sites to get information you need on companies and intended individuals.

Develop and Keep a Master Database

After long hours of compiling your targeted lists, this gold mine of intel, where should you keep it? How about on pieces of paper? How about in a file cabinet? How about in an excel spreadsheet on your computer? No? How about a Google Doc? The wisdom in effective and efficient prospecting is to have a complete and accurate MASTER DATABASE. This means having one major source for storing information on all contacts (suspects, prospects, customers, strategic contacts, vendors, partners, etc.) in one centralized place. Keeping a Master Database of all possible prospects gives you peace of mind knowing that all the information you have on a given prospect is consolidated in one place. Plus, having it all together ultimately saves you many hours. In compiling this Master Database, make sure that you pay attention to the little details, such as de-duping, having accurate, current information, and having consistent formatting of first and last names.

While some might say that keeping your Master Database in a spreadsheet is fine, I respectfully disagree. A Master Database should be housed in a CRM or Contact Management System. There are many reasons for this. First, this electronic format lets you retrieve your data anywhere you have Internet access (assuming the CRM is cloud-based or hosted). Second, it gives you the benefit of running detailed reports on the database with just a few clicks of the mouse. Third, it allows you to quickly import and export data from other lists, thereby more effectively merging duplicate records. Fourthly, using CRMs gives you the ability to send bulk email, bulk SMS, and build direct mailings. And finally, with the presence of over one hundred CRM options to choose from, the cost to purchase and maintain a cloud-based CRM can be a low as $25 per month, per user. Some CRM vendors like HubSpot and Zoho have free editions.

Pre-Call Research

Now that we know exactly who we are targeting, you have all their necessary contact information easily accessible in a CRM, we are ready to make contact, right? Not quite, there is still the matter of pre-call research. This is research you use to help you with relevance and personalization during your initial contact. In conducting pre-call research, you look to gain data and insights into a few key points, such as possible hot-button, industry trends, and economic landscape that might have a possible impact on this target's business.

We already know that people buy from people they like and/or who are like them. So in order to make this initial connection meaningful you need to conduct research to discover and find out what you have in common with the RPC. What are this person's interests? What school did they attend? What sports team do they follow? What causes do they support? Is anybody at your company already connected to your prospect on LinkedIn? Do you share a common LinkedIn group with your prospect? Has this company recently received a significant round of funding? Did the prospect just celebrate a special occasion? How about a birthday? Or a job promotion? Any intel that you can use and leverage to get past the guards of the prospects during your initial contact and pave the way to a meaning and open dialogue about issues, concerns, and challenges should be captured.

Ideas of Hot Buttons

What does he or she believe in? What business issues are of particular concern? There are some experts and many training programs that teach salespeople how to ask probing questions so that the prospect reveals his deepest pain. This can also be what keeps him up at night, to what his deepest desires are. While I have had great success in conducting this type of discovery, it also comes with a lot of teeth-pulling. It is not practical, and in my opinion somewhat naive, to believe that prospects will reveal intimate details on the first contact. So instead of trying to get this kind of data out of the prospect during the initial call, why not be armed with this intel prior to making contact? Doing so might even impress the contact, because you actually took the time to learn about their business. With the amount of personal data that a large number of prospects put on their social media profiles, getting this information has never been easier.

Just Enough Information

How much pre-call research is necessary? This depends upon the complexity of the sales. For transactional deals, very little pre-call research needs to be done and frankly may not even be necessary. The more complex the deal, the more expensive the offer, the longer the sales cycle, and the greater the number of decision-makers involved in the final purchase, the more information you need to ensure you have the best shot at closing. For the average deals, I use a method promoted by the company Inside Sales. This technique is called "3x3 Research."[4] The idea is that you spend three minutes gathering three specific pieces of information about your prospect before each call. Any more research is unnecessary for the majority of deals. Additionally, spending time researching could get in the way of contact time. Again, the amount of time you spend is determined by the level of understanding you need to have regarding this prospect.

Where to obtain this information

We live in an information revolution. Some might say an age of information overload. There is so much information about so many things, that it can be overwhelming. Be that as it may, access to this information is easier since the advent of the Internet. The pace of new content creation and the free access to that content does not seem to be slowing down anytime soon. You can look at a company's website. You can look at various directory listings and various social media sites. You can read the local business section of your newspaper. Incidentally, this last method has been part of the world of prospecting and selling for at least one hundred years. Also, you can attend networking events and simply talk to people, ask questions, and listen in on important conversations that might impact the types of business you target.

16: The Contact

Contact is the point where preparation and opportunity meet!

– JOHN HARVEY –

Once you know who your targets are, once you have all the contact information for making the outreach, the next question is *how* should you make contact? Meaning, **what method should you use to get in front of your suspect for the purpose of determining if there is a legitimate opportunity to do business?** Because minus the contact, how else will you know if your suspect has a problem, need, want, desire, goal, challenge, or pain that your products or services can help "fix" in some way? How will you know if the contact is a suspect or a true prospect? Additionally, what outreach methods will you deploy? Will you use the phones to make the outreach? Will you only use Social-Prospecting tools? How about SMS or even Net Prospecting? In the final analysis, effectively connecting with your contact requires you to use the right method or combination of contact methods. Effectively connecting also demands that you employ the optimal number of contact attempts as well as know the best time for contacting. There are various methods that you can use to get in front of your suspects for the purpose of determining if that contact (suspect really) is a prospect or not. Before getting into the discussion of each direct contact method, I first want to explore the *type* of contact you attempt – meaning is the contact attempt cold, warm, or hot?

What is Cold-Calling?

So much has been written about cold-calling. Some experts write about the "demise" or "death" of cold-calling. What seems to amaze me is that the very experts who write the obituary for cold-calling are the very ones who have little to no direct selling experience. More importantly, nor do they do any real prospecting to generate leads. Be that as it may, just what exactly is cold-calling?

Is cold-calling the process of calling someone who is not expecting your call-in order to initiate a sales conversation? Is cold-calling the process of calling someone who does not know you? What if the prospect does know something about you and your company, and you make an outreach (still an unexpected call), is that a cold call? What if you get a name from a customer or an associate in your network, and you call that person, is this cold-calling? What if you had the referrer person arrange a specific date and time for you to call the prospect? Is this a cold call? Wow! I know! Such complexity. But is this complexity necessary?

If you listen to the current debate between experts on traditional prospecting versus "new school" inbound marketing, it seems as though Social Selling is gaining a lot of traction. Consequently, it seems, on the surface, that the aforementioned level of complexity *is* necessary. Before writing this book, I would have said the same thing. Now, however, I think a little differently. In analyzing the temperature of an outreach, I have come to conclude that there are two factors that determine a call's degree of coldness. These two factors are best stated in the form of questions.

1. Is the outreach expected?
2. Does the prospect know you or know something about you?

I define **cold-calling as the process of making an unexpected, (unsolicited) outreach** to a contact regardless of whether they know you (or know of you), your company, your product, or your brand, with the goal of convincing them to do something differently. From this perspective, it doesn't matter whether they know you or not. Also it does not matter if they've had prior contact with you. Granted, an unexpected call to someone who knows you or with whom you have had prior contact is a much "warmer" call than calling someone unexpectedly who does not know you. Nonetheless, both types of outreaches are still cold-calling if you are contacting them unexpectedly. Why does this distinction matter? Because it helps you to anticipate the possible reactions of the suspect during the outreach and therefore are better prepared to handle such reactions skillfully and confidently.

Warm-Calling

If you think trying to understand "cold-calling" is difficult, try putting some meaning and understanding around "warm-calling." Be forewarned, this exercise might leave you with an equally throbbing headache. If you Google the term "warm-calling," you will find various meanings. I recall many years ago, when I was doing a joint workshop for a large insurance company with an on-staff sales trainer. This trainer commented that warm-calling meant you're calling a prospect with whom you've had some prior contact. At the time, I thought that definition seemed plausible. Just as I thought it was fair that some experts consider referral calls as warm-calling. For clarity, referral calling is when you reach out to someone who has been referred to you.

What if, however, this same referral is not expecting your call, or what if you don't have a pre-scheduled appointment? Is this call still warm? Some, might say yes. I, however, say no. No, is it not a warm call. It is still a cold-call. This is because essentially **a warm call is when the prospect is essentially expecting your call**. This call expectation on the prospect's part does not mean that you, the sales professional, necessarily knows whether or not the prospect has an immediate need or desire for your product. That would be another type of calling.

Hot-Calling

Over the years, I had not come across this term in a way that made sense to me with regard to how I use cold-calling and warm-calling. To recap, cold calling is when you are making "an unexpected call" to a prospect regardless of whether the prospects knows you or not; warm calling is when you are making "an expected call" to a prospect. But hot- calling, is an entirely different animal. Think about this. Is hot-calling when a you are calling someone who expects your call, but also has an immediate need for your product? Would this count as hot-calling? If so, how would you know this prior to making contact? Maybe you can make the assumption that all inbound leads are hot-calling. That is, the prospect has to reach out to you and you have a scheduled time to speak regarding their immediate needs. What about a scheduled call with a referred prospect who has an immediate need for your product? Is this hot-calling, as well? The answer is definitely YES!

Let's face facts. How many of us as sales professionals would love to spend most, if not all, of our time doing nothing but hot-calling? Sounds great right? Hold on! Like inbound leads or buyer-initiated contacts, hot calls do not happen as often as we would like. Nor do they happen in large enough quantities to fill a pipeline or close the requisite number of deals. For example, if you rely heavily on referral marketing to fill your funnel, you know that this method takes time to build and time to see the fruits of your labor. However, if you are in a sales role that is starved for business, then you can't rely on hot-calling to fill your funnel today. Otherwise, you will starve, or at the very least out of a job. You need to engage in either cold-calling or warm-calling or both first.

Here is another truth. As much as salespeople love hot-calling, they equally hate the coldest of cold calls. These are those types of outreach where the prospect is not expecting your call AND in which the prospect does not know you, your company, or your brand. Let's also acknowledge that calls of these type can be made warmer. Also, let's acknowledge the fact that there are some contact attempt methods that are less intrusive than others. These include emailing, social media, inmails and direct messages, and direct mails. These less intrusive methods may be leveraged to make the outreach warmer. Even if these less intrusive methods are used to make contact with a prospect, the attempt is still considered cold-calling.

Why is it important to understand the temperature of a call and the various types of outreaches? Because no matter what method you select, the outreach will always be cold if it is unexpected. This understanding also helps you handle the prospect's reaction skillfully and professionally. Plus, knowing this permits you to find other ways of making the call warmer or by leveraging less intrusive methods before using the more intrusive ones.

Making the Call Warmer

How can you make cold-calling work better? Initially, start out with less intrusive methods and move to more intrusive ones, all while setting the expectations for a follow-up call or visit. Additionally, you can and should use social media tools, such as inmails, direct messages, follows, retweets, tags as a means of making contact. Often times this approach is a less intrusive means of getting the suspect to begin to know who you are. Following the less intrusive method, then make a direct outreach via the phone, in person, or with an email. The contact still might not be expecting your call or visit, but at least the prospect will begin to know something about you, your company, your product, and your brand. This pre-branding, if you will, can be a big boost for whenever you make actual contact and begin to engage the potential buyer in a conversation. Remember, the best warm calls are when you have an introduction from someone your contact already knows and when you call someone who expects your call.

Persistence and Relentlessness

How many outreaches does it take to reach your prospect? Is it one? Is it two? What if you can't get in contact with your prospect by the fifth attempt? Should you give up and disregard the lead as unable-to-contact? Depending on your choice of method, the answer to this question might shock you. Before 2005, it took on average roughly three call attempts to reach a prospect. Today this number ranges between eight and thirteen depending on the source. That is, if you are using the phones as the contacting vehicle. For emails it can take up to four to five outbound emails to get a response from the prospect. For In-Person Prospecting that number tends to be about three. While these numbers might sound discouraging, the reality is that most prospects are extremely busy and doing more multitasking than ever before. This is particularly true for prospects in the B2B space. With overflowing email inboxes, the constant ringing of the phone, the incessant social media app notifications, and more, most successful connecting (meaning, you actually get in front of the prospect) requires you to attempt a considerable number of outreaches regardless of the contact method you might use. Thus, you need to develop the mindset and the expectation that no matter what, you will persist and not relent in your efforts to get in front of the prospect.

Can contact happen on the first attempt? Of course. Might it take twenty-five attempts? This is possible as well. If the opportunities are worth it, you will have to find a way to persist. Will you have some contacts in your list that may never be reached? Again, or course. Just because it might take twenty-five attempts, just because some contacts may forever be unreachable, it is best that you know these things ahead of time. This knowledge will help you be better prepared and not get discouraged or lose focus. Because if you are to build a sales pipeline ripe with qualified leads, then you cannot quit making the necessary outreaches. You must be relentless in your pursuit to get in front of your prospective buyer.

Prospecting Cadence

Contact attempt cadence (also known as sales cadence or prospecting cadence) is a schedule of prospecting activities that tell you when you should reach out to prospects. Because some leads respond better to calls, some prefer to respond to emails, and some to other methods, it is advisable to diversify your approach. Many inside sales organizations use a combination of phone calls, emails, and social media activities, while outside sales professionals might leverage a combination of phones calls, visits, emails, and direct mails. There is no perfect formula. There is no right cadence that fits all businesses and all sales professionals. It is therefore up to the sales professional and the sales leadership to determine what works best or has worked best (in the past) for certain prospects, and then use those methods in their cadence. It is also imperative to document and track all activities in the CRM so that your team can take the analytics and glean from it what is and is not working, thereby permitting the necessary modifying and scaling to take place.

Here is a sample cadence that I have used and taught in various forms over the years to much success. It consists of calls, emails, social media outreaches, direct mail, and visits. Be mindful that this cadence was designed for an inside B2B prospecting team.

Day 1: Call, LVM (leave voicemail) if no answer

Day 2: Call, LVM if no answer, send email

Day 3: Connect via social media

Day 4: Wait

Day 5: Call; LVM if no answer

Day 6: Call, LNM (leave no voicemail); send email

Day 7: Wait

Day 8: Connect via social media

Day 9: Wait

Day: 10: Send direct mail

Day 11-14 Wait

Day 15: If feasible, make a visit

Day 17: Repeat the cycle over again

Again, this is just one example of a cadence that has proven great results. It may or may not be effective for your process. A Google search on the term "sales cadence" can net you a plethora of other examples you might be able to use as the basis to build your own customized cadence.

Results of Prospecting Cadence

If you are successful in your attempts, then you will find yourself standing in front of the prospect, or on the other end of the line with the prospect. However, there are times when despite your best efforts, you just can't establish contact. When this happens what should you do? If you have exhausted your contact cadence, should you discard the record? In other words, treat it as uncontactable and move on from it? Possibly. However, if you believe that the timing was just not right, put the contact aside for a cycle or two, come back to it later and re-attempt to contact the prospect with the same or a modified cadence.

Gatekeepers

Consider this scenario. You developed a great script of what you will say when you get in contact with the desired party. You make the call (or you drop by) and *bam*! You get stopped by the gatekeeper or the receptionist. What should you do? Should you run out the building? Should you hang up the phone? Should you panic? What?

You might be surprised to learn that there are a number of sales professionals who do in fact panic and either hang up the phone or run out the building. Mostly this is due to not expecting to get stopped because they have not developed a plan for if or when this happens. These stoppers or gatekeepers can pop up no matter the choice of channel. It also can and does happen with a direct mail piece, an email, a fax, or even with an In-Person Networking event, (although rare in the latter's case). In order to be successful at getting in front of your prospect, you will either have to learn how to get through or go around the gatekeeper.

For clarity sake, I want to take a minute to define the term gatekeeper. Depending on your source, gatekeeper is the "locked door standing between you and the person you need to speak with."[1] It may be defined as "the person who has the authority or ability to control access to your intended target."[2] Or simply as someone in an organization that has a lot of influence and restricts access to information or people. Regardless of the particular definition, the reality is that unless you find a way through or around, you will not have the opportunity to contact and engage the suspect for qualification purposes.

Getting Past the Gatekeeper

A lot has already been written in this subject. Some so-called advice is just straight-out rude and out-right lying. Others are good but could be much better. What I will add to this conversation are four things to keep in mind when dealing with gatekeepers.

First, never be confrontational. It does not serve you well to return a bad attitude or unprofessional tone back to gatekeeper who might feel it is her right to treat you poorly. Remember, you need this person. It is not the other way around. Regardless of the tone or attitude you get from the gatekeeper you need to remain calm, cool, and professional. You may rightly think that you don't deserve to be spoken to or treated in any less than desirable way. And you may be right. However, do not, I repeat, *do not* attempt to return like for like. While you might win this exchange, you will definitely lose the war! You will lose any future chances of getting in front of the RPC. Plus, the RPC probably won't be willing to have an open, direct, and revealing conversation regarding their needs if it is found that you were rude and nasty to the gatekeeper.

Second, always treat the gatekeeper with respect. Regardless of the title the gatekeeper may have, these folks are humans too. They have jobs to perform. Because of the nature of the job, many receptionists might receive less than fair treatment from inside the organization, as well as from outside vendors and salespeople wanting to get an audience with the right person.

Third, don't lie or give false information. While outright lying may help you bypass the gatekeeper **this time**, it will typically not make for a successful ending. If the key individual finds out that you lied to get through to him, that contact will almost certainly terminate communication with you. Plus, lying forces you to remember what you said out of fear that you get caught. Thereby, you will find that lying takes more work to execute and maintain.

Finally, always attempt to get the gatekeeper on your side. You can and will accomplish a lot more if you get the gatekeeper in your camp. She may never be an internal champion for your product, but when done correctly, the gatekeeper can often help you achieve your goal of getting in front of the RPC.

Following these steps won't guarantee that you get through but doing the opposite will ensure failure. Or better yet, if you do manage to get through, you might already be tarnished with a negative image that needs counteracting. Also, remember that just because you did not get through this time, this does not mean that you won't next time. Following these steps increases the likelihood of getting through on subsequent outreaches.

Going Around the Gatekeeper

Okay, so you tried all the above-mentioned points. Yet, you are still unable to convince the gatekeeper to connect you with the RPC. Now you wonder what to do next. One very powerful way of going around the gatekeeper is the call into the organization ahead of time and when you get the auto-attendant message, press the prompt for sales. Once there, you are mostly likely going to be connected to another salesperson. Fabulously done! You can use the basis of commonality to elicit help from the prospect's salesperson to get to your designated contact and maybe even get some intel along the way.

A secondary way of going around the gatekeeper is to call when the gatekeepers are likely not working. Most gatekeepers work 8:00 a.m. to 5:00 p.m., with lunch around noon. You might find that you have much greater success in calling before or after the official working hours of the gatekeeper or during their lunch. At these times, you might just be connected directly to your desired contact. When this happens, when you are standing in front of your targeted buyer, when you are on the other line with your prospect, you have just accomplished the second major step in generating qualified prospects. Congrats!

Now what?

ENGAGEMENT

Loading...

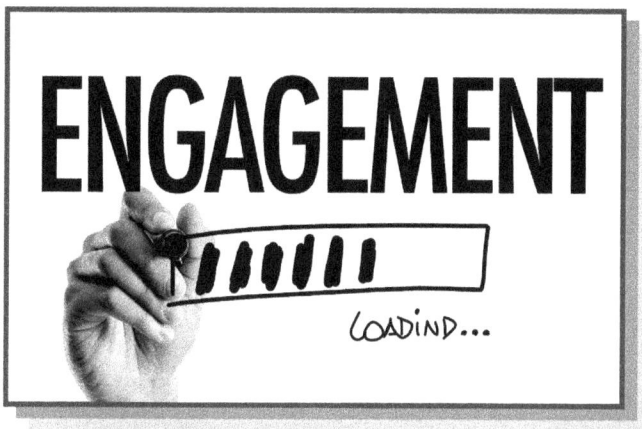

17: The Engagement

*When dealing with people, remember you're not dealing
with creatures of logic, but creatures of emotion.*

– DALE CARNEGIE –

Let's recap. You know exactly who you are targeting. You have compiled a list of potentials with contact details. If you were really successful in your research, you even gathered some contact information for the RPC. You have some background information that will help you personalize the initial contact. You have made a number of outreaches (phone calls, emails, a letter or two, maybe even reached out via social media). Remember, with some contacts you will be able to reach on your first attempt. While others (the majority) will require a number of attempts. If you persist long enough, if you are relentless in your pursuit, eventually you will reach all the prospects you desire, assuming you have accurate contact information.

When this happens, when you are in front of the prospect, what's next? What do you say to keep this person engaged until a meaningful discussion develops? What can you say to which the suspect willingly lets you pre-qualify her, so that you know if an opportunity to do business here really does exist?

There are a number of proven strategies that give you exactly what you are looking for. Our first task is to understand the purpose of the contact.

Purpose of the Contact

Is your goal to set an appointment? Is it to get some additional information? Is it to sell your product or service? If you sell a product that is transactional in nature (think of selling a single pen or selling tickets to the next charity ball sponsored by the Chamber of Commerce), then your initial contact and the ensuing conversations will be significantly different than that of a sales professional who sells a highly complex IT solution for large Fortune 500 companies. For full disclosure, all the information shared in this book up to this point are nuggets that any sales professional can use regardless of the complexity of the sales process they follow.

If this is the initial contact, then you will need to get into a conversation that ultimately determines whether there exists any customer pain for which your offering can help mitigate or eliminate completely (the ideal state). **Pain, in this sense, is the physical or psychological discomfort that a prospect experiences when he has unsolved problems, unresolved issues, unfulfilled desires, or unmet needs.**

For example, let's say that you are a company whose business is to set appointments for roughly 1,000 sales professionals from a variety of different organizations. Let's also say that your goal is to set one hundred appointments a day and thus 3,000 appointments monthly. With each appointment set you gross $100. Thus, when you hit your goal, you will gross $300,000 for the month. Not bad right? Stay with me, it gets better.

For the past ninety days, however, you have seen a steady decline in the number of appointments set. First month it was down by 10%; second month, the drop was 25%; now at the end of the third month, it is a whopping 35% drop in the number of appointments set. For clarity, this 35% drop equates to a loss of $105,000 for gross sales. And to add insult to injury, your clients are royally pissed and looking for immediate solutions.

This scenario is not meant to alarm you. It is just an example of what it means for a business to have pain present. Of course, when you make the initial contact you will not have this detailed information, unless you have done some research. You will undoubtedly need to engage the prospect in a way that induces the prospect to openly and willingly share crucial bits of information that will help you determine if you have a real, qualified lead. Rarely will this happen on the first contact. This depth of pain identification and analysis typically happens on the second contact. Therefore, the goal of the first contact is to greet and introduce yourself to the buyer and pique enough interest so that the prospect is willing to have a further conversation with you. It is this second conversation where you really determine if the opportunity to do business with this prospect is real or not. It is also the opportunity to discovery if what you offer benefits this prospect in a way that is different or better than what they might already be using now. Keep in mind that the engagement is not designed to sell. Instead, the engagement is designed to get the buyer to willingly open up and partake in a meaningful, interactive conversation with you, so that you have enough preliminary information to schedule a secondary meeting with them.

The Dreaded Interruption

One reason that cold-calling is difficult for many sales professionals is that it centers around the simple fact that when you call or drop in unexpectedly, you interrupt that prospect's day. If you are not expected, regardless of whether the contact knows you (or knows of you), it's an unscheduled interruption. Plain and simple! I think that most sales professionals intuitively know and accept this as true. Which is why so many sales professionals hate cold-calling.

However, what they fail to realize and accept is that this interruption happens, regardless of the type of outreach. Admittedly, if your outreach is an email, a direct mail, a social media InMail, or a direct message, then the prospect can decide whether or not to read your message. They can also decide when to read it. That stated, these softer outreaches are still interruptions. But these methods are not as direct as a telephone call, SMS message, or in-person visit, Therefore the potential vitriol that often happens with cold calls or a drop-in is much less with the former methods. That stated, even if you do make the initial outreach via a less intrusive method, at some point a call or face-to-face visit must happen to determine the validity of your prospect. When this happens, when you are finally in front of your contact, you have a limited amount of time to accomplish that goal.

How much time?

Depending on the source, you have anywhere from four to thirty seconds to greet, introduce, and pique enough interest so that the prospect agrees to another, much longer meeting. In his book *Way of the Wolf* [1] Jordan Belfort states that we have only about four seconds from the time you get into a call or meet the person face-to-face before the prospect decides if they should grant you any more of their time. Jordan further states, in this crucial four-second window, there are three things you must do if you want the prospect to perceive you as sharp as a tack, enthusiastic as hell, and an expert in your field. Yes, four seconds to accomplish all of this. Seems impossible, right? Well, luckily, if you mess up you still have another ten seconds to catch up. But if you don't get it right at that point, then you are screwed.

The Thirty-Second Rule

Most other experts are less restrictive than Jordan on this amount of time. As a matter of fact, my own experience as both a sales professional and a sales leader reveals that we have less than thirty seconds to make these points before the potential prospect dismisses, tunes-out, hangs-up, or walks away. Remember, during this time you need for the prospect to willingly stop what they are doing, listen to what you have to say (without hanging up on you before you have accomplished your objective) and engage you in a conversation sufficiently so that you accomplish your call objective.

At this point, you should be asking yourself the following questions:

1. Do I have enough time to share why this prospect should care about what I have to offer?

2. Do I have enough time to speak directly about how my product might benefit the prospect? Or how she will be better off by using my product?

3. Do I have enough time to share how useful my product is?

4. Do I have enough time to help the prospect determine if buying my product makes sense right now?

Unfortunately, no you don't. No, you don't have that much time.

There is an old saying (so old, I don't know who to quote) which states, "It is not what you say that is important, but how you say it." This might be true in normal everyday conversation, but if you want to get into a meaningful conversation with a prospect, then what you say and how you say it have equal weight. I had a sales manager earlier in my career tell me that if you are going to knock on the door, you damn well better have something really important to say. Otherwise, some prospects may make you regret having ever knocked on their door.

Let's look at the framework for effectively engaging the prospect.

The Greeting

As the first part of engagement, the greeting is nothing more than what you say when you first meet someone. Examples like: *Hi! Hello! Good morning! Good afternoon!* are really all there is to it. The greeting does not need to be long. It does not need to be complicated. It does not need to be otherworldly. The greeting just needs to be something that sounds simple, professional and direct.

The Introduction

After the greeting, the introduction is the next step. Like the greeting, the introduction is simple and straight forward. Here you are telling the prospect, who you are and what company you represent. No more, no less. If we put the two together, the greeting and the introduction, it would go something like this:

> *Hi (Mr./Ms. Prospect) My name is Christopher, I run a company called Bass Christopher & Associates.*

Again, like the greeting, the introduction is simple and direct. It does not need to be wordy. It does not need to be grand and elegant. Remember, you are still operating against time here, and you have other things to accomplish within this first thirty seconds.

The Purpose for the Outreach

The next item on this list is the purpose of the call. Why are you calling the prospect? Are you calling to book time on his calendar? To get some additional information? To sell on the spot? To qualify and then set an appointment? During my initial outreaches, my objective is to schedule or book time on my prospect's calendar. The nature of what I do requires a rather detailed conversation. Experience has taught me that such a call cannot and will not happen within the first call, as both the prospect and I need to prep for such a discussion. Whatever the purpose of the call, be upfront about it and state your reason. Remember, it does you no good to be passive or indirect about why you're reaching out. You are interrupting the prospect's day. Consequently, you have just a small window of time to get in, pique interest, and get done what you came to do.

Putting the greeting, the introduction and the purpose together, you might say something like:

> *Hi (Mr./Ms. Prospect) My name is Christopher, I run a company called Bass Christopher & Associates.*
>
> *The reason for the call (or the drop by) is to schedule a discovery call with you.*

The Because or The Pitch

Why should the prospect want to give you time on their calendar? Why would the prospect want to answer any questions you might have? At one of my earliest sales jobs, I was tasked with setting appointments for a group of senior sales reps. This objective was pretty straight forward. Get past the gatekeeper. Get the RPC on the line. Effectively introduce and pitch the company and then set an appointment for the prospect to meet with the senior reps within one week of the initial call. While the process was straightforward, my results were anything but straight.

Even though I was great at everything else, I struggled mightily with getting the person to agree to the appointment. It wasn't until I had a one-on-one coaching session with my sales manager that I learned I was missing one vital piece. **I was not giving the prospect valid reasons for why they should agree to an appointment with a senior rep.** He explains to me the research on *how* and *why* people grant requests. He told me that once I make a request I should immediately follow it up with my reasons for the request. Because requests with reasons are granted 50% times more than requests offered without any reasons. Again, a request followed with reasons for the request is granted 50% more than a request without reasons. Lesson learned. When stating the purpose for the call, also give reasons for why the prospect should agree to give you what you want.

In sales training sessions as well as sales books, you hear a lot about pitching. The constant refrain is that a great salesperson should always make sure that he has a great pitch. At networking meetings, you are likely to be asked to give a thirty- second or one- minute pitch. But what does this mean? What is a pitch?

In my practice, we look at pitching very differently. In its simplest from, a pitch is a brief statement that shares *why*. That is, why do customers do business with you. Why should the prospect care about what you do? Why is it important that the prospect grant you your request? Remember, to us the pitch is the reasons for the request. It gives the because.

An example of a pitch in conjunction with my introduction and greetings is as follows.

> *Hi (Mr./Ms. Prospect) My name is Christopher, I run a company called Bass Christopher & Associates.*
>
> *The reason for the call (or the drop by) is to schedule a discovery call with you.*
>
> *You see, we are experts at helping our clients overcome the biggest challenges to generating enough qualified prospects and increasing win rates.*
>
> *Now, I don't know if what we have to offer is the "right fit" for your company. This would require a discovery conversation. Here, I could learn more about your business, have you share with me your goals and from there determine what might be getting in the way of your achieving those goals.*

If you notice, the above framework covers three points: *Who* I am; *What* I do; and *Why* the prospect should care (or *Why* the prospect would want to grant my request). If the prospect is not suffering from either of the two pains articulated in my pitch, then this contact would not be a prospect. This structure is just one point to consider.

The delivery of message above is equally as important as the words you use. That is because the effectiveness of your message needs to move the prospect at two levels: the logical level and the emotional level. Logically prospects are moved to take action by the words we use. This include the reasons, the facts, and the figures that we use in our message. In contrast, prospects are moved emotionally to take action based on your tone and body language. It is only when you have effectively communicated both that you get the prospect to make a decision or take action. When prospects take action it is because, the verbal and nonverbal messages that we communicate speak specifically to their unique needs, wants, concerns, or desires. The simple point to all this. Make sure that you are delivering this message with energy and controlled enthusiasm.

The Next-Step

Many times, getting the prospect to commitment to any next step can be difficult. This next step is often referred to as a call-to-action (CTA). It is with the CTA that you determine the success of your initial call. Invariably, we train our clients that in order to get a next step (which is commitment from the prospect), they need to be assumptive to commit to the next step. If your next step is securing an appointment for the second meeting or call, you will be more effective in accomplishing this if you follow a couple of pointers.

First, when making the request, always have two very specific times slots available for the prospect to select. You should not make it the prospect's responsibility to look at his entire calendar and select a time. Instead you should select two times and let the prospect decide which of the two works better. Secondly, if neither of those times work for the prospect, ask the prospect if he prefers morning, afternoon or evening. Finally, ask the prospect to look at his calendar for the next five days and suggest a time that does work well for him. Putting this all together, it would look something like this:

> Hi (Mr./Ms. Prospect) My name is Christopher, I run a company called Bass Christopher & Associates.
>
> The reason for the call (or the drop by) is to schedule a discovery call with you.
>
> You see, we are experts at helping our clients overcome the biggest challenges to generating enough qualified prospects and increasing win rates.
>
> Now, I don't know if what we have to offer is the "right fit" for your company. This would require a discovery conversation. Such a call

would give me the opportunity to learn more about your business, have you share with me your goals and from there determine what might be getting in the way of your achieving those goals.

If this makes sense, how about we get together by phone (or in person) _____ (day) at _____ (time)?

The Prequalification

Often, the pre-contact research you conducted will not be enough to let you know if the prospect meets your basic factors for being an ideal client. For example, maybe you sell software and the company you represent has a user or license minimum, or you only sell to clients who have a certain type of accounting process, possibly one in which the processes for a particular function is in-house and not outsourced. Pre-Qualification (Pre-qual for short) is necessary, as it lets you know if the prospect meets the basic requirements to do business. You can do the Pre-qual either before you set the appointment or post setting the appointment. Many times, we train our clients to get the appointment first. During the appointment confirmation process, the sales professional can use a Pre-qual questionnaire to weed out those who don't fit the basic profile. It should be noted, that the purpose of executing this step (and all the preceding steps) is to segway from the pitch, to scheduling the appointment (or next step), to doing the pre-qualifications in a smooth, effective, and efficient way. Remember, the purpose of the pre-qualification is to determine if the prospect is someone whom you should have a further conversation with.

Ensure a High Show Rate

If your next step is to conduct the qualifying conversation in a subsequent meeting, and if your contact has passed your pre-qualification questions, then it is time to lock down the appointment. The goal here is to ensure there is a high degree of probability (not a guarantee) that the prospect will show up for the secondary meeting. Failure to lock-down the appointment will result in you having a lot of cancelled, no-show, or rescheduled appointments. Locking down the appointment involves confirming the details of the appointment (day, time, and location), identifying the reasons that might lead to the appointment not sticking, and getting confirmation that, short of those reasons happening, the appointment is solid. Locking down the appointment also entails getting acknowledgment and agreement that if these unforeseen reasons were to happen, the prospect will notify you ahead of time.

After the lock-down process you are just about done. You still need to send a post meeting calendar invite, along with some collateral material that help support the meeting, and at the same time contain valuable insights that the prospect can use. Finally, you must call or email the day before the appointment to confirm again. This double-confirmation might seem unnecessary, but you will find that such a process significantly increases your appointment show rate.

Let's recap. During your many contact attempts, you finally succeed in getting in front of your prospect. When this happens, you effectively greet, introduce, state your reason for the call, advance a call-to-action, maybe asked a few pre-qualification questions, and finally lock down the appointment. Yes! You are rolling now. You are almost at the finish line, almost at the point to where you can unequivocally say you have a real prospect for your sales pipeline. You are almost there. You just have to conduct one last meeting – the qualification meeting.

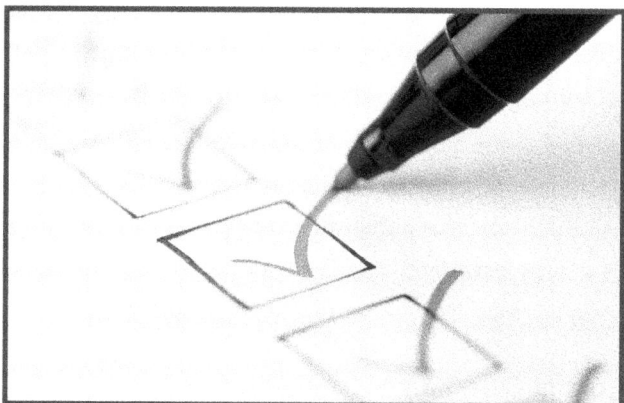

18: The Qualification

*Too many actors have run for office. There's one difference
between me and them; I know I'm not qualified.*

– JAMES GARNER –

I s the contact – your lead – qualified or not? Do you have a suspect or prospect? This is the million-dollar question, because it's what the selling process is based on. While selling is the very foundation that our modern economies are driven by, no sale can happen, no sale *does* happen until a qualified lead has been identified. Everything that we have covered up to this point shows you how to get into a qualifying conversation to determine if the contact, if the target, is a prospect or just a mere suspect. At the end of the day, it does you no good to have leads in your pipeline if you are not proactively qualifying those leads. It does you no good to have suspects instead of real prospects. It does you a ton of good to always have qualified leads that you advance along the sales process and ultimately close.

Of course, there will be a number of leads that are not YET qualified, but that can become qualified over time. With these leads, you want to keep and nurture them. There will also be some contacts that are not qualified and never will be. Whenever you discover these unqualified or disqualified leads, it is to your benefit to discard them from your funnel. This determination of whether the lead is qualified, needs nurturing, or should be discarded, is all made possible by the all-important qualifying conversation (also known as the discovery or needs analysis). As this type of a call often gets very intrusive and detailed, you first have get the prospect's approval to provide you with those details. To do so requires that you learn how to master the art of questioning.

The Power of the Question

He who asked the questions is the one who controls and dictates the flow and direction of a conversation. This is a statement that is drilled into every student of selling. Yet, for all of its merits, few sales professionals truly follow this advice. It's unfortunate, because contrary to popular opinion, we don't learn anything new while we speak. It is only by listening that we truly learn. The key to listening is to first ask questions that lead the prospect to share with you information that we must have to fully qualify the opportunity.

Even Socrates, the great Greek Philosophy (470-399 BC) knew the wisdom and the power of asking questions. His technique, called the Socratic method, is based on a system of questioning others and oneself in order to arrive at the truth. It is said that Socrates' aim in this line of questioning "was to get to the foundations of his students' and colleagues' views until a contradiction was exposed, thus proving the fallacy of the initial assumption."[1] While many law schools in the U.S. employ the Socratic method when training law students, it is my belief that many modern-day systems of selling and their processes of asking questions are inspired by the Socratic method, as well.

Leveraging the power of questions is not just about asking questions. It is also about making sure the manner and tone of the questioning is more akin to the style of a doctor or a trusted advisor, one who uses questions to dig for information so that she can properly diagnose the problem and make the best recommendations. The style that you don't want to emulate is that of an attorney cross examining a witness or an investigator conducting a criminal interrogation. You are out to help the prospect, not entrap, manipulate or harm.

The Agenda

As the qualifying conversation is typically the second call with a potential prospect, it is common to use an agenda to properly set the stage and expectations of the meeting. From a general standpoint, an agenda is nothing more than a formal outline or declaration of things to be done during a meeting.[2] In the context of prospecting and qualifying, this agenda is much more. One very effective use of agendas is the one employed by sales professionals who follow the Sandler System of Selling. This method was introduced to me by one of my assistant sales manager nearly 5 years. This method is so effective that I have used it to this very day to great results.

The method in question is called the Upfront Contract (UFC).[3] The intention is to start with the end in mind while concurrently minimizing the tendency of haphazardly conducting meetings. The UFC generally has five elements. These include:

1. The purpose of the meeting
2. The sales professional's agenda for the meeting
3. The prospect's agenda for the meeting
4. The expected outcome of the meeting
5. The estimated duration of the meeting

I learned the hard way many years ago that making a contract and sticking to it, gives the sales professional the ability to control the selling process and focus on the specific needs of the prospect. With a set agenda for every meeting, sales professionals can take the element of surprise out of the selling process.

The Opening

After the agenda, it's time to get down to business. Yet, you don't want to rush in too fast or too hard. You want to ease into the conversation so that you encourage the prospect to drop his natural defenses. Unless they drop their guard, you will not be able to identify pain, impact, and other intimate and private details. One way to get the person to open up and have a conversation with you is to get them to talk about the things that mean the most to them. In his famous book *How to Win Friends and Influence People* Dale Carnegie states that if you get people to talk about themselves, or what interests them, they will open up to you and share many personal details.[4]

Specific Questions to Ask

If you have done the pre-call research, then you can ask clarifying questions such as:

1. I see that you started your company about five years ago. What lead to you develop this particular business?

2. Your company is primarily a service business. If your best customer were to walk in here today what would they look?

3. Why do customers choose you over the competitor? Or why do they elect to change rather than stay with the status quo?

The above questions are examples of open-ended conversation starters that you can use to get the prospect to speak about the things they are most interested in. When they speak about things that are near and dear to them, that is when their defenses drop.

The Needs Analysis

Once the prospect talks freely and openly, now you can ask more probing questions as their walls lower due to the common bond that you have just developed. This is where you now dig for some pain, impact, possible solutions, and other factors that ultimately determine any decisions regarding a new solution. Remember, during this process you want to move from less to more intrusive questions that make the prospect vulnerable and at times emotional. Prospects are more willing to go down this road with you after you have established trust, competency, and likeability.

Framework for the Discovery

During this intel-gathering session, you may wonder what are the outcomes of the questions you should be asking? Below are examples of the information you should gather during this call.

1. **Understand the business**. Here the goal is to get the prospect to talk about the most essential and important parts of her business. If you've

done your pre-call research, you should know which questions to ask and which parts of the business to focus on. The number of questions asked here should be no more than two or three.

2. **Determine their goals, wants and/or desires**. Businesses are driven by goals. The success of any business is its ability to reach its goals. This is true of consumers as well. Underlying those goals are wants and desires. If you want to generate high-quality prospects, then you must get the prospect to share with you certain key goals, as well as the underlying wants and desires that define and shape those goals.

3. **Know the process that your solution helps**. Once you know what the prospect's key goals are, and what wants and desires those goals are based upon, it is time to explore the specific processes that the business uses to achieve its goals. For example, I help my clients with generating qualified prospects and winning sales, so I will naturally ask questions, specific questions, about any and all processes that involve prospecting and selling.

4. **Identify their current challenges or pain**. During my discussion on the Goals of Prospecting, I mentioned that during prospecting you look for prospects with unfulfilled goals you can help them attain; desires you can help them fulfill; pain you can help them ease; challenges you can help them address; needs you can help them satisfy; or problems you can help them solve. In other words, you are looking for *their pain*. You are looking for gaps in current versus targeted. This is critically important, because if they don't have pain, then they won't have a compelling reason to make changes.

5. **Get clear on the impact of their pain**. The greater their pain, the greater their desire to relieve that pain. Your goal is not to manufacture pain, but rather to magnify it so that the prospect acknowledges the negative effectives of the pain, both emotionally and verbally, leaving no room for denial of what will continue if the pain (the problem) is not addressed. When impact is verbalized by the prospect, this often becomes the single most compelling reason for why a change MUST happen sooner rather than later. It is your

job to get the prospect to verbalize what the current and potential impacts are to the keeping the status quo.

6. **Recognize their current approach and past attempts**. If someone has been in denial for years, once they emotionally and verbally acknowledge the problem, they feel compelled to do something about it. The question then becomes *what?* What, if anything, is the prospect doing to address their problem? What have they done in the past? Explore or evaluate the effectiveness of the current and past approach, the reasons why those options where selected, and why they don't work now.

7. **Offer a new situation**. Now that you've identified the problem (or pain), its negative impacts, and the attempts that have been made in the past to address it, you must now explore the possible solutions. Ask questions like the magic wand or other what if questions. *If you had a magic wand, what changes would you make right now? What would you do differently today knowing what you now know? When will you do it? Do you believe that this self-proposed solution will finally address the problem?*

8. **End with a decision-making qualification**. At this point you know whether the target is a suspect or a prospect. Now, you must find out how you can ultimately win the business. Look at factors such as the timeframe for making the decisions and who the key players are that make the decisions. You also want to know other important factors such as the distinction between what the prospect considers to be *must-haves* versus *wish-list* items, Ask the prospect to share either his either budget or ability to pay.

Post Needs Analysis Decision

By now it is clear, or at least should be clear at the conclusion of this discovery, that you have a prospect and thus should begin to move into the selling phase. But if it is not fully a prospect, should you nurture it so that it becomes qualified over time? Or should the lead just be discarded as there is no way this suspect will ever become a prospect? Even if the latter is the case, you still have the possibility of getting referrals from the contact. Whatever you decide, qualified now, not qualified yet, it is clear that generating leads for the sales pipeline requires a lot of thought, a lot of planning, and a lot of execution. Be that as it may, generating leads is just the first step. You now have to work on transitioning from a prospecting mode to a selling mode.

Winning the Deal

The selling mode consists of product selection, solution design, solution presentation, answering questions, overcoming barriers and objections, negotiating, getting agreement, and finally collecting payment. As tempting as it might be for me to discuss each of these steps I will save that discussion for a future book. So, stay tuned.

Final Thoughts

We have come full circle. We started with a discussion on the importance of sales, and how the success of businesses and entire economies depend upon sales. We also examined how (as important as sales are to business) sales can't happen until a sales professional possesses a qualified lead or prospect. From that point on, we built a compelling case as to why it is important to look at prospecting differently than how lay people (and even some sales professionals) view it. I then asked the question, *if one is to prospect, then what is the best way of generating a pipeline full of qualified opportunities?* I called this situation the bottomless prospect pipeline – bottomless in the sense that it has no end and is constantly being refilled.

From there we looked at the various communication channels that a sales professional could leverage to generate these high-quality prospects. And we explored in great detail the four major steps that a sales professional must execute in order to be successful at generating qualified leads. These steps include: **Finding, Contacting, Engaging, and Qualifying** the prospect. It is important to recognize that these steps are in play regardless of the communication channel. While we have come full circle, generating qualified leads is just the start.

The next major objective that followed is to convert those qualified leads into paying customers. Also, a decision must be made regarding what to do with those leads that while not fully qualified now can become qualified over time through some nurturing. Additionally, the long-term goal of any new business acquisition is to grow the long-term value of the business and to expand each new customer's lifespan with your company. All great topics, which are, unfortunately, outside the scope of this book.

In writing this book, there were a number of other topics that I could have included but didn't. I am talking about: more script examples, or how product knowledge generates high quality prospects, or tips how to overcome barriers and objections that emerge in your pursuit to qualify a prospect. I elected not to include those other subjects deliberately based on a few factors.

First, there are so many other great books on prospecting and sales that I saw no purpose in duplicating works that had already been done. That is, unless I took a different approach. Secondly, when I got started in sales nearly twenty years ago, there was no book like the one you have in your hands right now to help me get a practical understanding of what prospecting is, the importance of doing it, and how I could go about generating leads (at least not without the super level of complexity that far too many books foster).

In the final analysis, I hope that you use this book for what is it, which is a source, a guide, or as stated by the title, a playbook as you go about your job of prospecting and keeping your sales pipeline full. I know that my overall mission in helping all those in a sales role significantly impact their revenue targets will not be fully complete until the other volumes covering the aforementioned topics are discussed. Nevertheless, at least this present book should significantly increase your capacity to generate more qualified leads regardless of your skill level or years of experience. This book will undoubtedly aid you in accepting that fact that you don't have to like prospecting. But you do, however, have to do it well, and at a very high level, if you plan to tackle the crippling problem of anemic sales pipelines. A problem that plagues far too many well-intentioned sales professionals. If you embrace this reality and conduct yourself accordingly, then my goal in writing this particular book will be achieved.

I am always curious how my speeches, trainings, and coaching sessions impact my client's performance. This curiosity is ever-present with the writing of this, my first book. So please let me know how the information contained between these pages helped you fix whatever prospecting challenges you had. Thereby allowing you to win more sales. Please share your stories, both the successes and the struggles, by either emailing me directly at *christopher@ basschristopher.com*, or reaching out to me on any of my social media sites, or even calling my office directly at 818.722.1240. I do promise to reply to every communication sent.

Until the next book, remember ABP. **Always Be Prospecting!**

About the Author

Christopher Bass is a sales expert with over twenty years of experience in every possible facet of sales. He speaks, writes, trains, and coaches companies and sales professionals on how to overcome the biggest challenges associated with generating qualified prospects and winning more sales efficiently and faster.

Over his long career, Christopher has occupied various roles ranging from business development rep, closer, account manager, sales manager, sales director, and head sales trainer for many companies. If there is a sales position, Christopher has been there and done that. Having the insight and expertise that only comes with experience, Christopher has faced both great successes and huge failures in pursuit of top sales goals. While the successes validate what works, the failures are equally important in that they teach us what not to do and why.

Christopher's unique background in theory and application has not only benefited him as a sales rep with a quota, but also has helped hundreds of other sales reps of varying roles and experience, all of whom he has had the great fortune to train, coach, and manage.

With field-tested, real-world experience, academics, and intensive self-study under his belt, Christopher has the expertise to help your sales team WIN MORE sales today!

To learn more about how Christopher can help your organization overcome the key challenges that prevent your sales team from winning more sales or to book him to speak at your next event, call 818.722.1240 or email *christopher@basschristopher.com.*

Notes

Chapter 1: Sales

1. http://www.businessdictionary.com/definition/sales.html.
2. Mike Kaplan, *Secrets of a Master Closer: A Simpler, Easier, and Faster Way to Sell Anything to Anyone, Anytime, Anywhere*. Master Closers, Inc., 2012.
3. *National Association of Sales Professional*, https://www.nasp.com.
4. *National Sales Network*, http://salesnetwork.org.
5. Grant Cardone, *Be Obsessed or Be Average*. New York: Penguin Random House, LLC, 2016.
6. Mark Cuban Interview, *Bloomberg*, June 14, 2013, https://www.youtube.com/watch?v=KYneLGRTgy8.
7. "What is Social Selling," *LinkedIn*, https://business.linkedin.com/sales-solutions/social-selling/what-is-social-selling.

Chapter 2: Lead Generation

1. "Definition of Lead Generation," *Marketo*, https://www.marketo.com/lead-generation/.
2. "Definition of Promotion," *American Marketing Association Online Dictionary*, http://www.marketing-dictionary.org/Marketing+Communications.

Chapter 3: Prospecting

1. Richard Stephens, "Cold Calling is Dead: 15 New Prospecting Strategies Salespeople Should Use," *Hubspot*, https://blog.hubspot.com/sales/lead-generation-alternatives-to-cold-calling.
2. David Mattson, *The Sandler Rules: 49 Timeless Selling Principles and How to Apply Them*. Beverly Hills, CA: Pegasus Media World, 2009.
3. Steve Schiffman, *Cold Calling Techniques (That Really Work) 5th Edition*. Avon, MA: Adams Media, 2003.

4.   Ava Frost, "75 Mind-Blowing Sales Statistics That Will Help You Sell Smarter in 2018," *Hubspot,* https://blog.hubspot.com/sales/sales-statistics.
5.   Jeb Blount, *The Ultimate Guide for Starting Sales Conversations and Filling the Pipeline by Leveraging Social Selling, Telephone, E-Mail, and Cold Calling.* Hoboken, NJ: John Wiley & Sons, 2015.

Chapter 4: Eight Steps to Becoming Great

1.   Tim Grover, *Relentless: From Good, to Great, to Unstoppable.* New York: Scribner, 2014.
2.   Jeb Blount, *The Ultimate Guide for Starting Sales Conversations and Filling the Pipeline by Leveraging Social Selling, Telephone, E-Mail, and Cold Calling.* Hoboken, NJ: John Wiley & Sons, 2015.

Chapter 6: Tele Prospecting

1.   Gary Stauble, "The 30-Minute Rule for Overcoming Call Reluctance," https://www.eremedia.com/fordyce/the-30-minute-rule-for-overcoming-call-reluctance/.
2.   Jordan Belfort, *Way of the Wolf: Straight Line Selling: Master the Art of Persuasion, Influence, and Success.* New York: North Star Way, 2017.
3.   Alex Orton, "5 Ways to Get Leads to Call Back," *InsideSales.com,* https://www.insidesales.com/insider/inside-sales/5-ways-to-get-leads-to-call-back-in-2013/.

Chapter 7: Email Prospecting

1.   "Email Statistics Report 2017-2021," *The Radicati Group,* https://www.radicati.com/wp/wp-content/uploads/2017/01/Email-Statistics-Report-2017-2021-Executive-Summary.pdf.
2.   Patricia Reaney, "Email Connects 85 Percent Of The World; Social Media Connects 62 Percent," *Huffpost,* https://www.huffingtonpost.com/2012/03/27/email-connects-the-world_n_1381854.html.
3.   Craig Smith, updated by, "85 Interesting Emails Statistics and Facts (2017) By the Numbers," *DMR,* https://expandedramblings.com/index.php/email-statistics/.
4.   Laura Vanderkam, "Stop Checking Your Email, Now," *Fortune,* http://fortune.com/2012/10/08/stop-checking-your-email-now/.

5. Ava Frost, "75 Mind-Blowing Sales Statistics That Will Help You Sell Smarter in 2018" *Hubspot,* https://blog.hubspot.com/sales/sales-statistics.

6. Greg Sterling, "Mobile Devices Drive 66 Percent Of Email Opens – Report," *Marketing Land,* https://marketingland.com/34-percent-email-opens-now-happen-pc-83277.

7. Kendra Lee, "Is the Glimpse Factor Stalling Your Emails?" *KLAGroup,* http://www.klagroup.com/is-the-glimpse-factor-stalling-your-emails/.

8. *Small Business Ideas Blog,* http://www.smallbusinessideasblog.com/find-email-addresses.

9. https://blog.beamery.com/find-email-addresses/.

10. https://www.saleshandy.com/blog/email-finding-tools/.

11. https://www.process.st/find-email-address/.

12. Lindsay Kolowich, "The FREE Beginner's Guide to Email Marketing," *Hubspot,* https://blog.hubspot.com/marketing/email-marketing-beginners-guide.

Chapter 8: SMS Prospecting

1. "Number of mobile phone users worldwide from 2013 to 2019 (in billions)," *Statista,* https://www.statista.com/statistics/274774/forecast-of-mobile-phone-users-worldwide/.

2. *BlueDot Mobile,* https://www.facebook.com/bluedotmobile/photos/pb.117768891602834.-2207520000.1475215889./1115023278544052/?type=3&theater.

3. "Data Never Sleeps 5.0," *Domo,* https://www.domo.com/learn/data-never-sleeps-5.

4. "SMS Marketing Wallops Email with 98% Open Rate and Only 1% Spam," *Mobile Marketing Watch,* https://mobilemarketingwatch.com/sms-marketing-wallops-email-with-98-open-rate-and-only-1-spam-43866/.

5. David Mielach, "Americans Spend 23 Hours Per Week Online, Texting," *Business News Daily,* https://www.businessnewsdaily.com/4718-weekly-online-social-media-time.html.

6. Nathan Eddy, "Businesses Texting Grows More Widespread," *eWeek,* http://www.eweek.com/small-business/businesses-texting-grows-more-widespread.

7. "Text Message Marketing, The New Kid On The Block [Infographic]," *Slicktext,* https://www.slicktext.com/blog/2014/02/text-message-marketing-the-new-kid-on-the-block-infographic/.

8.   Adam Small, "How to Use SMS to Win Love, Leads, Revenue," *Martech,* https://martech.zone/text-messaging/.

9.   Michael Cusdan, "Top 10 Benefits of SMS Marketing," *SimplyCast Blog,* https://www.simplycast.com/blog/top-10-benefits-sms-marketing/.

10.   "6 Benefits of SMS Marketing" *Smart Insights,* https://www. smartinsights.com/mobile-marketing/sms-marketing/6-benefits-sms-marketing/.

11.   "Marketing with 98 Percent Read-Rate and 10 More Compelling Stats," *Adobe Blog,* https://theblog.adobe.com/marketing-with-98-percent-read-rate-and-10-more-compelling-stats/.

12.   "Can I text my customers legally?" *Tatango,* https://www.tatango.com/blog/can-i-text-message-my-customers-legally/.

13.   Nick Hedges, "3 Tips for Leveraging SMS In the Sales Process," *Velocify Blog,* https://velocify.com/blog/3-tips-for-leveraging-automated-text-messaging-in-the-sales-process/.

Chapter 9: Direct Mail Prospecting

1.   "Direct Mail Statistics," *DMA,* https://thedma.org/marketing-insights/marketing-statistics/direct-mail-statistics/.

2.   Steve Slaunwhite, "Does Prospecting with Direct Mail Work?" *AWAI Online,* http://www.awaionline.com/2017/06/does-prospecting-with-direct-mail-work/.

3.   Ishbel Macleod, "Infographic: consumers more likely to deal with direct mail immediately compared to email," *The Drum,* http://www.thedrum.com/news/2013/10/23/infographic-consumers-more-likely-deal-direct-mail-immediately-compared-email.

4.   Henry Adaso, "10 Mind-Blowing Direct Mail Statistics," *DMN3,* https://www.dmn3.com/dmn3-blog/10-mind-blowing-direct-mail-statistics-and-what-they-mean.

5.   Craig Simpson *The Direct Mail Solution: A Business Owner's Guide to Building a Lead-Generating, Sales Driving, Money Making Direct-Mail Campaign.* Irvine, CA: Entrepreneur Press, 2014.

Chapter 10: Fax Prospecting

1.   "History of the Fax (from 1843 to Present Day)," *FaxAuthority,* https://faxauthority.com/fax-history/.

2.   Paul Freeman-Powell, "It's 2015. Why are people still using fax?" *Crosby Fax,* https://www.crosbyfax.com/blog/2015/04/its-2015-why-are-people-still-using-fax/.

3.   Patrick Phelps, "Uses of Faxes in Business," *Bizfluent,* https://bizfluent.com/list-6771987-uses-faxes-business.html.

4.   "Faxing Via Email Saves Valuable Time in Prospecting for New Clients and Closing Deals," *Mbox,* https://www.mbox.com.au/fax-resources/fax-via-email-time.

5.   Amrit Igcse, "Pros and Cons of Using a Fax Machine," *Amrit's Igcse Blog,* http://athan96049.weebly.com/pros-and-cons-of-using-a-fax-machine.html.

6.   "Junk Fax Prevention Act of 2005," *Wikipedia,* https://en.wikipedia.org/wiki/Junk_Fax_Prevention_Act_of_2005.

Chapter 11: In-Person Prospecting

1.   Glen Shelton, "THE COMPLETE GUIDE TO DOOR-TO-DOOR COLD KNOCKING," *Lead Heroes,* https://www.leadheroes.com/the-complete-guide-to-door-to-door-cold-knocking/.

2.   Robert Hartline, "3 Tips for Tracking Door to Door Sales," *Call Proof,* http://callproof.com/2015/07/07/tracking-door-to-door-sales/.

Chapter 12: Net Prospecting

1.   Bob Burg, *Endless Referrals; Network Your Everyday Contacts into Sales, 3rd Edition.* New York: McGraw-Hill, 2006.

2.   Ivan Misner and Brian Hilliard, *Networking Like a Pro, 2nd Edition.* Irvine, CA: Entrepreneur Press, 2017.

3.   Joe Girard, *How to Sell Anything to Anybody.* New York: Touchstone, 2006.

Chapter 13: Social Prospecting

1.   "How Can Marketers Benefit from Using Social Selling Tools," *Emarketer,* https://www.emarketer.com/Article/How-Marketers-Benefit-Using-Social-Selling-Tools/1014298.

2.   https://www.csoinsights.com/.

3.   "What is Social Selling," *LinkedIn,* https://business.linkedin.com/sales-solutions/social-selling/what-is-social-selling.

4.   Kathleen Schaub, "Social Buying Meets Social Selling: How Trusted Networks Improve the Purchase Experience," *IDC,* https://business.linkedin.com/content/dam/business/sales-solutions/global/en_US/c/pdfs/idc-wp-247829.pdf.

5.   Katie Kind, "Social Selling and the death of the traditional salesperson?" *Digital Leadership Associates,* http://www.social-experts.net/social-selling-and-death-traditional-salesperson/.

6.   Shannon Belew, *The Art of Social Selling,* New York: AMACOM, 2014.

7.   Cheryl Connor, "Sharing Too Much Will Cost You," *Forbes,* https://www.forbes.com/sites/cherylsnappconner/2012/10/19/sharing-too-much-itll-cost-you/#7ab5a7664125.

8.   "The consequences of oversharing on social networks," *Reputation Defender Blog,* https://www.reputationdefender.com/blog/privacy/consequences-oversharing-social-networks.

9.   Shannon Belew, *The Art of Social Selling,* New York: AMACOM, 2014.

10.   Antony Maina, "20 Popular Social Media Sites Right Now," *Small Business Trends,* https://smallbiztrends.com/2016/05/popular-social-media-sites.html.

11.   Gagan Mehra, "105 Leading Social Networks Worldwide," *Practical Ecommerce,* https://www.practicalecommerce.com/105-leading-social-networks-worldwide.

12.   Prit Kallas, "Top 15 Most Popular Social Networking Sites and Apps [January 2018]," *DreamGrow,* https://www.dreamgrow.com/top-15-most-popular-social-networking-sites/.

13.   Linkedin Social Selling Index.

14.   "The Klout Score," *Klout,* https://klout.com/corp/score.

15.   Ruxandra Mindruta, "Marketing: Top 15 Free Social Media Monitoring Tools," *Brandwatch.com,* https://www.brandwatch.com/blog/top-10-free-social-media-monitoring-tools/.

16.   Shannon Belew, *The Art of Social Selling,* New York: AMACOM, 2014.

Chapter 14: Which Channel is Better?

1.   https://www.investopedia.com/terms/p/portfolio.asp.

Chapter 15: The Find

1.   https://www.ama.org/resources/Pages/Dictionary.aspx.

2.   "Shotgun Marketing," *Marketing-Schools.org,* http://www.marketing-schools.org/types-of-marketing/shotgun-marketing.html.

3.   "Hunting Elephants Definition," *Investopedia,* https://www.investopedia.com/terms/h/hunting-elephants.asp#ixzz51omoSlku.

4.   Ken Krogue and Steve Richard, "Cold Calling is Dead, Thanks to LinkedIn," *InsideSales,* http://static.insidesales.com/assets/pdf/ebook-cold-calling-is-dead-thanks-to-linkedin-08-2014.pdf.

Chapter 16: The Contact

1.   http://smallbusiness.chron.com/gatekeeper-marketing-36870.html.

2.   http://www.businessdictionary.com/definition/gatekeeper.html.

Chapter 17: The Engagement

1.   Jordan Belfort, *Way of the Wolf: Straight Line Selling: Master the Art of Persuasion, Influence, and Success.* New York: North Star Way, 2017.

Chapter 18: The Qualification

1.   "The Socratic Method," *The University of Chicago Law School,* https://www.law.uchicago.edu/socratic-method.

2.   https://www.merriam-webster.com/dictionary/agenda.

3.   "Upfront Contract," *Sandler Blog,* https://www.sandler.com/search/site/upfront%20contracts.

4.   Dale Carnegie, *How to Win Friends and Influence People.* New York: Simon & Schuster, 1936.

www.ingramcontent.com/pod-product-compliance
Lightning Source LLC
Chambersburg PA
CBHW071653210326
41597CB00017B/2199